BEYOND TRAGEDY

BOOKS BY REINHOLD NIEBUHR

The Irony of American History
Faith and History
Discerning the Signs of the Times
The Children of Light and the Children of Darkness
The Nature and Destiny of Man (ONE VOLUME EDITION)
Christianity and Power Politics
Beyond Tragedy
An Interpretation of Christian Ethics
Moral Man and Immoral Society

Beyond Tragedy

ESSAYS ON THE CHRISTIAN
INTERPRETATION OF HISTORY

By

Reinhold Niebuhr

NEW YORK
CHARLES SCRIBNER'S SONS

CONTENTS

vii

CONTENTS

PREFACE

THE CHAPTERS of this book are sermonic essays elaborating one theme in various aspects. The theme is Christianity's dialectical conception of the relation of time and eternity, of God and the world, of nature and grace. It is the thesis of these pages that the biblical view of life is dialectical because it affirms the meaning of history and of man's natural existence on the one hand, and on the other insists that the centre, source and fulfilment of history lie beyond history.

Christianity must therefore speak both a "yes" and a "no" to naturalistic philosophies. It affirms them inasfar as they insist on the meaningfulness of historical existence. It refutes them inasfar as they believe that the temporal process explains and fulfils itself. In the same way it affirms the distinction between time and eternity in mysticism, and rational dualistic philosophies, but rejects their denial of the significance of the historical process. In the biblical view each moment of history stands under and in eternity but neither exhausts nor fulfils the eternal.

Inasfar as orthodox Christianity has developed this

biblical view into a supernaturalism which conceives of two discrete realms of being, the natural and the supernatural, it represents a petrifaction of a more mythical and dialectical biblical thought. It may not be unjust to regard this development as the consequence of Greek rationalism upon the more mythical and Hebraic biblical thought, in which the depth of eternity in time is conceived of in terms which sacrifice rational consistency to profundity of religious insight. An ancillary theme of these essays is therefore the necessary and perennially valid contribution of myth to the biblical world view. This subject is dealt with specifically in the first essay, "As Deceivers, Yet True," and incidentally in some of the other essays.

The idea of a meaningful history does not, however, explain the actual content of meaning. It is the thesis of these essays that the Christian view of history passes through the sense of the tragic to a hope and an assurance which is "beyond tragedy." The cross, which stands at the centre of the Christian worldview, reveals both the seriousness of human sin and the purpose and power of God to overcome it. It reveals man violating the will of God in his highest moral and spiritual achievements (in Roman law and Jewish religion) and God absorbing this evil into Himself in the very moment of its most vivid expression. Christianity's view of history is tragic insofar as it recognizes evil as an inevitable concomitant of even the highest spiritual enterprises. It is beyond tragedy inasfar as it does not regard evil as inherent in existence itself but as finally under the dominion of a good God.

Most of the material of these essays was first used in sermons preached in college and university chapels. As the sermons were not written at the time of their delivery their subsequent transcription has somewhat altered their form from sermons to essays. Their content has also been slightly altered in the interest of the unity of the whole.

REINHOLD NIEBUHR.

Union Theological Seminary,
New York City,
August, 1937.

One:
AS DECEIVERS,
YET TRUE

But in all things approving ourselves as the ministers of God, in much patience, in afflictions, in necessities, in distresses, in stripes, in imprisonments, in tumults, in labours, in watchings, in fastings; by pureness, by knowledge, by longsuffering, by kindness, by the Holy Ghost, by love unfeigned, by the word of truth, by the power of God, by the armour of righteousness on the right hand and on the left, by honour and dishonour, by evil report and good report; as DECEIVERS and YET TRUE; as unknown, and yet well known; as dying, and, behold, we live; as chastened, and not killed; as sorrowful, yet alway rejoicing; as poor, yet making many rich; as having nothing, and yet possessing all things.

II Corinthians 6:4–10.

I: AS DECEIVERS, YET TRUE

AMONG the paradoxes with which St. Paul describes the character, the vicissitudes and the faith of the Christian ministry, the phrase "as deceivers yet true" is particularly intriguing. Following immediately after the phrase "by evil report and good report" it probably defines the evil reports which were circulated about him as charges of deception and dishonesty. This charge is refuted with his "yet true." But the question arises why the charge is admitted before it is refuted. Perhaps this is done merely for the sake of preserving an unbroken line of paradoxical statements. If this be the case, a mere canon of rhetorical style has prompted a very profound statement. For what is true in the Christian religion can be expressed only in symbols which contain a certain degree of provisional and superficial deception. Every apologist of the Christian faith might well, therefore, make the Pauline phrase his own. We do teach the truth by deception. We are deceivers, yet true.

The necessity for the deception is given in the primary characteristic of the Christian world view. Christianity does not believe that the natural, temporal and historical world is self-derived or self-explanatory. It believes that the ground and the fulfilment of existence lie outside of existence, in an eternal and divine will. But it does not hold, as do many forms of dualism, that there is an eternal world separate and distinct from the temporal world. The relation between the temporal and the eternal is dialectical. The eternal is revealed and expressed in the temporal but not exhausted in it. God is not the sum total of finite occasions and relationships. He is their ground and they are the creation of His will. But, on the other hand, the finite world is not merely a corrupt emanation from the ideal and eternal. Consequently the relation of time and eternity cannot be expressed in simple rational terms. It can be expressed only in symbolic terms. A rational or logical expression of the relationship invariably leads either to a pantheism in which God and the world are identified, and the temporal in its totality is equated with the eternal; or in which they are separated so that a false supernaturalism emerges, a dualism between an eternal and spiritual world without content and a temporal world without meaning or significance.

I

Before analysing the deceptive symbols which the Christian faith uses to express this dimension of eternity in time, it might be clarifying to recall that artists are forced to use deceptive symbols when they seek to portray two dimensions of space upon the single dimension of a flat canvas. Every picture which suggests depth and perspective draws angles not as they are but as they appear to the eye when it looks into depth. Parallel lines are not drawn as parallel lines but are made to appear as if they converged on the horizon; for so they appear to the eye when it envisages a total perspective. Only the most primitive art and the drawings made by very small children reveal the mistake of portraying things in their true proportions rather than as they are seen. The necessity of picturing things as they seem rather than as they are, in order to record on one dimension what they are in two dimensions, is a striking analogy, in the field of space, of the problem of religion in the sphere of time.

Time is a succession of events. Yet mere succession is not time. Time has reality only through a meaningful relationship of its successions. Therefore time is real only as it gives successive expressions of principles and powers which lie outside of it. Yet every suggestion of the principle of a process must be expressed in terms of the temporal process, and every idea of the God who is the ground of the world must be expressed in some term taken from the world. The temporal process is like the painter's flat canvas.

5

It is one dimension upon which two dimensions must be recorded. This can be done only by symbols which deceive for the sake of truth.

Great art faces the problem of the two dimensions of time as well as the two dimensions of space. The portrait artist, for instance, is confronted with the necessity of picturing a character. Human personality is more than a succession of moods. The moods of a moment are held together in a unity of thought and feeling, which gives them, however seemingly capricious, a considerable degree of consistency. The problem of the artist is to portray the inner consistency of a character which is never fully expressed in any one particular mood or facial expression. This can be done only by falsifying physiognomic details. Portraiture is an art which can never be sharply distinguished from caricature. A moment of time in a personality can be made to express what transcends the moment of time only if the moment is not recorded accurately. It must be made into a symbol of something beyond itself.

This technique of art explains why art is more closely related to religion than science. Art describes the world not in terms of its exact relationships. It constantly falsifies these relationships, as analysed by science, in order to express their total meaning.

II

The Christian religion may be characterised as one which has transmuted primitive religious and artistic myths and symbols without fully rationalising them. Buddhism is much more rational than Christianity. In consequence Buddhism finds the finite and temporal world evil. Spinozism is a more rational version of God and the world than the biblical account; but it finds the world unqualifiedly good and identical with God. In the biblical account the world is good because God created it; but the world is not God. Every Christian myth, in one way or another, expresses both the meaningfulness and the incompleteness of the temporal world, both the majesty of God and his relation to the world.

We are deceivers yet true, when we say that God created the world. Creation is a mythical idea which cannot be fully rationalised. It has therefore been an offense to the philosophers who, with the scientists, have substituted the idea of causality for it. They have sought to explain each subsequent event by a previous cause. Such an explanation of the world leads the more naïve thinkers to a naturalism which regards the world as self-explanatory because every event can be derived from a previous one. The more sophisticated philosophers will at least, with Aristotle,

7

seek for a first cause which gives an original impetus to the whole chain of causation. But such a first cause does not have a living relationship with the events of nature and history. It does not therefore account for the emergence of novelty in each new event. No new fact or event in history is an arbitrary novelty. It is always related to a previous event. But it is a great error to imagine that this relationship completely accounts for the new emergence. In both nature and history each new thing is only one of an infinite number of possibilities which might have emerged at that particular juncture. It is for this reason that, though we can trace a series of causes in retrospect, we can never predict the future with accuracy. There is a profound arbitrariness in every given fact, which rational theories of causation seek to obscure. Thus they regard a given form of animal life as rational because they can trace it historically to another form or relate it in terms of genus and species to other types of life. Yet none of these relationships, whether historical or schematic, can eliminate the profound arbitrariness of the givenness of things.

It is therefore true, to account for the meaningfulness of life in terms of the relation of every thing to a creative centre and source of meaning. But the truth of creation can be expressed only in terms which outrage reason. Involved in the idea of creation is the concept of making something out of nothing. The *Shepherd* of Hermas declares "First of all believe that God is one, who created and set in order all things and caused the universe to exist out of nothing." This was the constant reiteration of Christian belief, until in very modern times it was thought possible to substitute the idea of evolutionary causation for the idea of creation. The idea of creation out of nothing is profoundly ultrarational; for human reason can deal only with the stuff of experience, and in experience the previous event and cause are seen, while the creative source of novelty is beyond experience.

The idea of creation relates the ground of existence to existence and is therefore mythical rather than rational. The fact that it is not a rational idea does not make it untrue or deceptive. But since it is not rational it is a temptation to deceptions. Every mythical idea contains a primitive deception and a more ultimate one. The primitive error is to regard the early form in which the myth is stated as authoritative. Thus the Christian religion is always tempted to insist that belief in creation also involves belief in an actual forming of man out of a lump of clay, or in an actual creative activity of six days. It is to this temptation that biblical literalism succumbs. But there is also a more ultimate source of error in the mythical statement of religious belief. That is to

9

regard the relation of each fact and event in history to a Divine Creator as obviating the possibility of an organic relation to other facts and events according to a natural order. By this error, which Etienne Gilson[1] calls "theologism," Christian theology is constantly tempted to deny the significance of the natural order, and to confuse the scientific analysis of its relationships. At the rise of modern thought Malebranche developed a doctrine of "occasionalism" which expressed this error of Christian theology in its most consistent form. But it has been a persistent error in Christian thought and one which arises naturally out the mythical statement of the idea of creation. The error is analogous to that of certain types of art which completely falsify the natural relations of objects in order to express their ultimate significance.

We are deceivers, yet true, when we say that man fell into evil. The story of the fall of man in the Garden of Eden is a primitive myth which modern theology has been glad to disavow, for fear that modern culture might regard belief in it as a proof of the obscurantism of religion. In place of it we have substituted various accounts of the origin and the nature of evil in human life. Most of these accounts, reduced to their essentials, attribute sin to the inertia of nature, or the hypertrophy of impulses, or to the defect of reason (ignorance), and thereby either ex-

[1] In his *Unity of Philosophical Experience.*

plicitly or implicitly place their trust in developed reason as the guarantor of goodness. In all of these accounts the essential point in the nature of human evil is missed, namely, that it arises from the very freedom of reason with which man is endowed. Sin is not so much a consequence of natural impulses, which in animal life do not lead to sin, as of the freedom by which man is able to throw the harmonies of nature out of joint. He disturbs the harmony of nature when he centres his life about one particular impulse (sex or the possessive impulse, for instance) or when he tries to make himself, rather than God, the centre of existence. This egoism is sin in its quintessential form. It is not a defect of creation but a defect which becomes possible because man has been endowed with a freedom not known in the rest of creation.

The idea of the fall is subject to the error of regarding the primitive myth of the garden, the apple and the serpent, as historically true. But even if this error is not committed, Christian thought is still tempted to regard the fall as an historical occurrence. The fall is not historical. It does not take place in any concrete human act. It is the presupposition of such acts. It deals with an area of human freedom which, when once expressed in terms of an act, is always historically related to a previous act or predisposition. External descriptions of human behaviour are therefore always deterministic. That is the deception into which those are betrayed who seek to avoid the errors of introspection by purely external descriptions of human behaviour. What Christianity means by the idea of the fall can only be known in introspection. The consciousness of sin and the consciousness of God are inextricably involved with each other. Only as the full dimension of human existence is measured, which includes not only the dimension of historical breadth but the dimension of trans-historical freedom, does the idea of the fall of man achieve significance and relevance.

It is interesting to note that Christian theology has usually regarded the fall as an historical occurrence, even when it did not accept the primitive myth of the Garden of Eden. It therefore spoke of a perfection before the fall as if that too were an historical era. Even the sophisticated dialectical theology of Barth and his school speaks of the perfection before the fall as historical, and consequently elaborates a doctrine of human sinfulness which approaches, and sometimes surpasses, the extremism of the historic doctrine of total depravity. The perfection before the fall is an ideal possibility which men can comprehend but not realise. The perfection before the fall is, in a sense, the perfection before the act. Thus we are able to conceive of a perfectly distinterested justice; but when we act our own achievements will fall short of this standard. The rationalists always assume that, since men are able to conceive of perfect standards of justice, such standards will be realised as soon as all men become intelligent enough to conceive them. They do not realise that intelligence offers no guarantee of the realisation of a standard, and that the greatest idealists, as well as the most cynical realists or the most ignorant victims of an immediate situation, fall short in their action; nor that such falling short arises not simply from the defect of the mind but from an egoistic corruption of the heart. Self intrudes itself into every ideal, when thought gives place to action. The deceptions to which the idea of the fall give rise are many; and all of them have been the basis of error at some time or other in the history of Christian theology. We are deceivers, yet true in clinging to the idea of the fall as a symbol of the origin and the nature of evil in human life.

III

We are deceivers, yet true, when we affirm that God became man to redeem the world from sin. The idea of eternity entering time is intellectually absurd. This absurdity is proved to the hilt by all the theological dogmas which seek to make it rational. The dogmas which seek to describe the relation of God the Father (the God who does not enter history) and God the son (the God of history) all insist that the

13

Son is equal to the Father and is yet not equal to Him. In the same way all the doctrines of the two natures of Christ assert that he is not less divine for being human and temporal and not less human and temporal for being fully divine. Quite obviously it is impossible to assert that the eternal ground of existence has entered existence and not sacrificed its eternal and unconditioned quality, without outraging every canon of reason. Reason may deal with the conditioned realities of existence in their relationships and it may even point to the fathomless depth of creativity out of which existential forms are born. But it cannot assert that the Divine Creator has come into creation without losing His unconditioned character. The truth that the Word was made flesh outrages all the canons by which truth is usually judged. Yet it is the truth. The whole character of the Christian religion is involved in that affirmation. It asserts that God's word is relevant to human life. It declares that an event in history can be of such a character as to reveal the character of history itself; that without such a revelation the character of history cannot be known. It is not possible to arrive at an understanding of the meaning of life and history without such a revelation. No induction from empirical facts can yield a conclusion about ultimate meaning because every process of induction presupposes some canon and criterion of meaning. That is why metaphysical systems which pretend to arrive at ultimate conclu﹒sions about the meaning of life are either covert theologies which unconsciously rationalise some reve-lation, accepted by faith; or they merely identify rationality with meaning, a procedure which forces them into either pantheism or acosmism. They must either identify the world with God on the supposition that temporal events, fully understood in all their relationships, are transmuted from finiteness and contingency into an unconditioned totality; or they must find the existential world evil in its finiteness because it does not conform in its contingent, existen-tial relationships to a rational idea of unity.

For Christian faith the world is neither perfect nor meaningless. The God who created it also reveals Himself in it. He reveals Himself not only in a general revelation, that is, in the sense that His crea-tion is His revelation; but in a special revelation. A general revelation can only point to the reality of God but not to His particular attributes. A theology which believes only in a general revelation must inevitably culminate in pantheism; because a God who is merely the object of human knowledge and not a subject who communicates with man by His own initiative is something less than God. A knowl-edge of God which depends only upon a study of the behaviour of the world must inevitably be as flat as the knowledge of any person would be, which de-

15

pended merely upon the observation of the person's behaviour. The study of human behaviour cannot give a full clue to the meaning of a personality, because there is a depth of freedom in every personality which can only communicate itself in its own "word." That word may be related to an analysis of behaviour and become the principle of interpretation for the analysis. But it is not the consequence of the analysis. Without such a word the picture of any personality would be flat, as the interpretations of the divine which eliminate revelation are flat.

In Christian thought Christ is both the perfect man, "the second Adam" who had restored the perfection of what man was and ought to be; and the Son of God, who transcends all possibilities of human life. It is this idea which theology sought to rationalise in the doctrines of the two natures of Christ. It cannot be rationalised and yet it is a true idea. Human life stands in infinity. Everything it touches turns into infinity. Every moral standard, rigorously analysed, proves to be no permanently valid standard at all short of perfect and infinite love. The only adequate norm of human conduct is love of God and of man, through which all men are perfectly related to each other, because they are all related in terms of perfect obedience and love to the centre and source of their existence. In the same way all evil in human life is derived from an effort to transmute finite values into infinities, to seek infinite power, and infinite wealth and infinite gratification of desire. There is no sharp line between the infinity in man and the infinity beyond man and yet there is a very sharp line. Man always remains a creature and his sin arises from the fact that he is not satisfied to remain so. He seeks to turn creatureliness into infinity; whereas his salvation depends upon subjecting his creaturely weakness to the infinite good of God. Christ, who expresses both the infinite possibilities of love in human life and the infinite possibilities beyond human life, is thus a true revelation of the total situation in which human life stands. There is every possibility of illusion and deception in this statement of the Christian faith. Men may be deceived by the primitive myth of the Virgin Birth and seek to comprehend as a pure historical fact, what is significant precisely because it points beyond history. Or they may seek to explain the dogma of the Incarnation in terms which will make it an article in a philosophical creed. Such efforts will lead to varied deceptions; but the deceptions cannot destroy the truth of the Incarnation.

Yet the revelation of God in the Incarnation is not of itself the redemption. Christianity believes that Christ died to save men from sin. It has a gospel which contains a crucifixion as well as an incarnation, a cross as well as a manger. This doctrine of the atoning death of the Son of God upon the cross has

17

led to many theological errors, among them to theories of substitutionary atonement which outrage the moral sense. There is in fact no theory of the atonement which is quite as satisfying as the simple statements of the vicarious death of Christ in the Gospels. This may mean that faith is able to sense and appropriate an ultimate truth too deep for human reason. This is the foolishness of God which is wiser than the wisdom of men. The modern world has found not only the theories of atonement but the idea of atonement itself absurd. It rebelled not only against theories of a sacrifice which ransomed man from the devil's clutches or of a sacrifice which appeased the anger of a vindictive divine Father; it regarded the very idea of reconciliation between God and man as absurd.

The reason for this simple rejection of the Christian drama of salvation lies in the modern conception of human nature, rather than in any rejection of the theological absurdities attached to the idea of Christ's atoning death. Modern man does not regard life as tragic. He thinks that history is the record of the progressive triumph of good over evil. He does not recognise the simple but profound truth that man's life remains self-contradictory in its sin, no matter how high human culture rises; that the highest expression of human spirituality, therefore, contains also the subtlest form of human sin. The failure to

18

recognise this fact gives modern culture a non-tragic conception of human history. To recognise this fact, and nothing more, is to reduce human history to simple tragedy. But the basic message of Christian faith is a message of hope in tragedy. It declares that when the Christ, by whom the world was made, enters the world, the world will not receive him. "He came unto his own and his own received him not." Human existence denies its own deepest and most essential nature. That is tragic. But when that fact is understood, when men cease to make the standards of a sinful existence the norms of life but accept its true norm, even though they fail to obey it, their very contrition opens the eyes of faith. This is the Godly sorrow that worketh repentance. Out of this despair hope is born. The hope is simply this: that the contradictions of human existence, which man cannot surmount, are swallowed up in the life of God Himself. The God of Christian faith is not only creator but redeemer. He does not allow human existence to end tragically. He snatches victory from defeat. He is Himself defeated in history but He is also victorious in that defeat.

There are theologies which interpret this article in the Christian creed as if life were really pure tragedy, but for the atoning love of Christ. But the fact is that the atoning death of Christ is the revelation of ultimate reality which may become the prin-

ciple of interpretation for all human experience. It is
not a principle yielded by experience, but it is ap-
plicable to experience and validated by it. It is an
actual fact that human life, which is always threatened
and periodically engulfed by the evil which human
sin creates, is also marvellously redeemed by the transmutation of evil into good. This transmutation is not
a human but a divine possibility. No man can, by
taking thought, turn evil into good. Yet in the total
operations of providence in history this transmutation
occurs. The Christian faith consequently does not defy
the tragic facts of human existence by a single victory
over tragedy; nor does it flee the tragedy of temporal
existence into a heavenly escape. These forms of the
Christian faith are deceptions.

Most profoundly the atonement of Christ is a
revelation of what life actually is. It is tragic from
the standpoint of human striving. Human striving
can do no better than the Roman law and the Hebraic
religion, both the highest of their kind, through
which the Lord was crucified. Yet this crucifixion
becomes the revelation of that in human history which
transcends human striving. And without this revelation, that which is beyond tragedy in life could not
have been apprehended. Without the cross men are
beguiled by what is good in human existence into a
false optimism and by what is tragic into despair. The
message of the Son of God who dies upon the cross,

20

of a God who transcends history and is yet in history, who condemns and judges sin and yet suffers with and for the sinner, this message is the truth about life. It cannot be stated without deceptions; but the truths which seek to avoid the deceptions are immeasurably less profound. Compared to this Christ who died for men's sins upon the cross, Jesus, the good man who tells all men to be good, is more solidly historical. But he is the bearer of no more than a pale truism.

We are deceivers, yet true, when we declare that Christ will come again at the last judgment, that he who was defeated in history will ultimately triumph over it, will become its judge and the author of its new life. No doctrine of Christianity has led to more deceptions and illusions than the hope of the second coming of Christ. This doctrine has been so frequently appropriated and exploited by sectarian fanatics that the church has been a little ashamed of it. We have made even less of the apocalyptic literature into which Hebraic prophecy culminated and in which Christ was nurtured. The imagery of this literature is so extravagant, and at times so fantastic, that Christian thinkers have been content, on the whole, to leave it alone. Yet the doctrine of Christ's second coming involves all the profoundest characteristics of the Christian religion. It is this doctrine which distinguishes Christianity both from naturalistic utopianism and from Hellenistic otherworldiness. In it the Christian hope of the fulfilment of life is expressed paradoxically and dialectically, holding fast to its essential conception of the relation of time to eternity. History is not regarded as meaningless, as in Greek thought, particularly in later neo-Platonism. For this reason the realm of fulfilment is not above history, in some heaven in which pure form is abstracted from the concrete content of historical existence. The realm of fulfilment is at the end of history. This symbolises that fulfilment both transcends and is relevant to historical forms. The end of history is not a point in history.

The chronological illusion, that it is a point in history, so characteristic of all myths which point to the trans-historical by a symbol of time, is particularly fruitful of error in the doctrine of the second coming. It has led to fantastic sectarian illusions of every type. Yet it is significant that the dispossessed and disinherited have been particularly prone to these illusions, because they were anxious to express the Christian hope of fulfilment in social as well as in individual terms. Sectarian apocalypticism is closely related to modern proletarian radicalism, which is a secularised form of the latter. In both, the individualism of Christian orthodoxy is opposed with conceptions which place the corporate enterprises of mankind, as well as individuals, under an ultimate judg-

22

ment and under ultimate possibilities of fulfilment. In these secular and apocalyptic illusions the end of time is a point in time beyond which there will be an unconditioned society. But there is truth in the illusions.

The more bourgeois version of this illusory apocalypticism is the idea of progress in which the unconditioned ground of history is explicitly denied, but an unconditioned fulfilment in terms of infinite duration is implicitly affirmed. The Kingdom of God, as the absolute reign of God, is transmuted into a principle of development, immanent in history itself. Against such a conception Christian thought is forced to maintain as rigorous opposition as against dualistic otherworldliness. The ultimate fulfilment of life transcends the possibilities of human history. There is no hope of overcoming the contradictions, in which life stands, in history. But since these contradictions are not the consequence of mere finiteness and temporality, but the fruits of human freedom, they are not overcome merely by translating the temporal into the eternal. Since they persist in all human striving, fulfilment is not a human but a divine possibility. God must overcome this inescapable contradiction.

Therefore it is Christ who is both the judge of the world and the author of its fulfilment; for Christ is the symbol both of what man ought to be and of what God is beyond man. In Christ we have a revela-

23

tion of both the human possibilities which are to be fulfilled and the divine power which will fulfil them. In Christ, too, we have the revelation of the significance of human history and of the ground of its meaning which transcends history.

We are therefore deceivers, yet true, when we insist that the Christ who died on the cross will come again in power and glory, that he will judge the quick and the dead and will establish his Kingdom. We do not believe that the human enterprise will have a tragic conclusion; but the ground of our hope lies not in human capacity but in divine power and mercy, in the character of the ultimate reality, which carries the human enterprise. This hope does not imply that fulfilment means the negation of what is established and developed in human history. Each moment of history stands under the possibility of an ultimate fulfilment. The fulfilment is neither a negation of its essential character nor yet a further development of its own inherent capacities. It is rather a completion of its essence by an annihilation of the contradictions which sin has introduced into human life.

Two:
THE TOWER
OF BABEL

And the whole earth was of one language, and of one speech. And it came to pass, as they journeyed from the east, that they found a plain in the land of Shinar; and they dwelt there. And they said one to another, Go to, let us make brick, and burn them thoroughly. And they had brick for stone, and slime had they for mortar. And they said, Go to, let us build us a city, and a tower, whose top may reach unto heaven; and let us make us a name, lest we be scattered abroad upon the face of the whole earth.

And the Lord came down to see the city and the tower, which the children of men builded. And the Lord said, Behold, the people is one, and they have all one language; and this they begin to do: and now nothing will be restrained from them, which they have imagined to do. Go to, let us go down, and there confound their language, that they may not understand one another's speech.

So the Lord scattered them abroad from thence upon the face of all the earth: and they left off to build the city. Therefore is the name of it called Babel; because the Lord did there confound the language of all the earth: and from thence did the Lord scatter them abroad upon the face of all the earth.

Genesis 11:1–9.

THE TOWER
OF BABEL

I

THE essential truth in a great religious myth cannot be gauged by the immediate occasion which prompted it; nor apprehended in its more obvious intent. The story of the Tower of Babel may have been prompted by the fact that an unfinished temple of Marduk in Babylon excited the imagination of surrounding desert people, who beheld its arrested majesty, to speculate on the reason for its unfinished state. Its immediate purpose may have been to give a mythical account of the origin of the world's multiplicity of languages and cultures. Neither its doubtful origin nor the fantastic character of its purported history will obscure its essential message to those who are wise enough to discern the permanently valid insights in primitive imagination.

The Tower of Babel myth belongs to the same category of mythical fancies as the Promethean myth, though the two are independent and not derived from each other. They both picture God as being jealous of man's ambitions, achievements and pretensions. The modern mind, which has exchanged the

27

wooden-headed literalism of orthodoxy for a shallow rationalism, can find no validity in the idea of a jealous God. It either does not believe in God at all, or the God of its faith is so very kind and fatherly as to be really grandmotherly. A jealous God expresses the primitive fear of higher powers from which the modern man feels himself happily emancipated. Yet the idea of a jealous God expresses a permanently valid sense of guilt in all human striving. Religion, declares the modern man, is consciousness of our highest social values. Nothing could be further from the truth. True religion is a profound uneasiness about our highest social values. Its uneasiness springs from the knowledge that the God whom it worships transcends the limits of finite man, while this same man is constantly tempted to forget the finiteness of his cultures and civilisation and to pretend a finality for them which they do not have. Every civilisation and every culture is thus a Tower of Babel.

The pretensions of human cultures and civilisations are the natural consequence of a profound and ineradicable difficulty in all human spirituality. Man is mortal. That is his fate. Man pretends not to be mortal. That is his sin. Man is a creature of time and place, whose perspectives and insights are invariably conditioned by his immediate circumstances. But man is not merely the prisoner of time and place. He touches the fringes of the eternal. He is not content to be merely American man, or Chinese man, or bourgeois man, or man of the twentieth century. He wants to be man. He is not content with his truth. He seeks *the* truth. His memory spans the ages in order that he may transcend his age. His restless mind seeks to comprehend the meaning of all cultures so that he may not be caught within the limitations of his own.

Thus man builds towers of the spirit from which he may survey larger horizons than those of his class, race and nation. This is a necessary human enterprise. Without it man could not come to his full estate. But it is also inevitable that these towers should be Towers of Babel, that they should pretend to reach higher than their real height; and should claim a finality which they cannot possess. The truth man finds and speaks is, for all of his efforts to transcend himself, still his truth. The "good" which he discovers is, for all of his efforts to disassociate it from his own interest and interests, still his "good." The higher the tower is built to escape unnecessary limitations of the human imagination, the more certain it will be to defy necessary and inevitable limitations. Thus sin corrupts the highest as well as the lowest achievements of human life. Human pride is greatest when it is based upon solid achievements; but the achievements are never great enough to justify its pretensions. This pride is at least one aspect of what Christian orthodoxy means by "original sin." It is not so much an inherited corruption as an inevitable taint upon the spirituality of a finite creature, always enslaved to time and place, never completely enslaved and always under the illusion that the measure of his emancipation is greater than it really is.

II

Lest the casual observer should be tempted to regard this defect in human spirituality as a harmless vagary, as an unavoidable failure of a limited reason fully to understand its limits, it becomes necessary to point out that the tragic self-destruction of civilisations and cultures, records of which abound in the annals of human history, are partially caused by this very defect. Plato and Aristotle could see history as the rise and fall of various city-states, but they regarded the city-state itself as the final form of political organisation. Yet it was the lack of wide social cohesion and the intra-Greek anarchy of this city-state organisation which proved to be the Achilles heel of Greek civilisation. The city-state was not a final or perfect social organisation. It was merely an expression of Greek particularism. Greek slavery probably contributed as much to the decline of Greek life as its inter-state anarchy. Inter-class wars added complications to the confusion of Greek political life. Yet both Plato and Aristotle regarded the class structure of their society as written into the eternal order of things.

Roman civilisation came as near to being co-terminous and identical with civilisation as such, as any social structure in the western world. The *Pax Romana* was something more than merely a peace enforced by Roman arms. But it was something less than the pure peace and justice of which Roman idealists boasted. The most characteristic cultural achievement of Roman civilisation was Roman stoicism. Roman stoicism was a perfect tower of Babel, for it partly transcended and partly sanctified the imperfect justice of Roman law. In the thought of Cicero stoic universalism and Roman imperialism were not quite identical but sufficiently so to allow the latter to enjoy the spiritual prestige of the former.

The most universal civilisation of Christian history was the medieval, feudal social structure which flowered in the thirteenth century in Europe. The moral and political authority of the Roman pontiffs checked the anarchy of morally autonomous political and national groups, and gave medieval Europe a political and social unity which it has since sought vainly to restore. The basic presuppositions of the Christian religion as interpreted from Augustine to Aquinas gave the cultural life of the continent common standards which were brilliantly elaborated in its literature, painting and architecture. This was a "Christian" civilisation in its own estimation. But it was also a Tower of Babel. It failed to realise that it was also primarily a landlord's civilisation which had carefully woven the peculiar economic interests of feudal aristocrats into the fabric of Christian idealism. Its theory of the "just price" sought to set a religio-moral check upon economic greed. But the theory of the just price was the expression of a consumer's economy at the expense of producers, the aristocrats being the consumers and the city artisans the producers. In the same way its rigorous prohibition of usury was ostensibly the application of a scriptural ideal to the problem of borrowing and lending. It was enforced only as long as the landed gentry were primarily borrowers and not lenders of money.

The very character of a Tower of Babel, and the primary cause of its always tragic history is that its limitations, and its pretentious disregard of those limitations, are not seen from the inside, *i.e.*, by those groups who have compounded partial insights and particular interests with eternal and universal values. Thus the landlords never discovered, and have not discovered yet, that their civilisation was less than Christian. The class which discovered this and which finally brought this Tower of Babel down was the class of merchants, business men, artisans and bankers who had been disregarded in the organisation of medieval life. The city grew up under the protection of the castle wall and, in spite of the oppression of the castle's power, finally acquired a power great enough to destroy the castle. But the lord protested to the end that he was protecting not his civilisation but civilisation as such, against the bolshevist of his day: the business man.

The final act of this tragedy is being enacted today in Spain where an anachronistic feudalism is perishing amidst the terrible passions and fratricidal conflicts of a civil war. Roman Catholic Christianity, the traditional instrument of the feudal Tower of Babel, refuses to the very last to admit that the civilisation which it has built is something less than a Christian civilisation. Thus the Roman Pope, referring to the Spanish conflict in his Christmas message of 1936, declared: "Whosoever seeks to portray the Church of Christ, custodian of divine promises and by divine mandate teacher of the peoples, as an avowed enemy of prosperity and progress, such a one is not only no builder of a prosperous future for humanity and his own country; on the contrary he is destroying the most effective and decisive means of defense against dreaded evils, and he is, even though he know it not, working with those against whom he believes and boasts that he is fighting."

The merchants who built our new social order were convinced that religion was primarily an instrument of social injustice, and that it always gave an unjustified halo of sanctity to the partial and relative values of a particular society. Thus bourgeois society, with the business man, rather than the landed aristocrat as the source of its most significant social power, was essentially rationalistic and irreligious. "You have built your ladders to heaven," declared Cosimo de Medici, a typical spirit of the eighteenth century; "we will not seek so high nor fall so low." Cosimo's simile fits the Tower of Babel aspect of medieval civilisation admirably. But it also contains the foundations of a new tower in which reason and science perform the function once performed by traditional religion.

Bourgeois society imagines itself free of prejudices. Its cultural ideal is that of a presuppositionless science. It believes that its social ideals of liberty, equality and fraternity are the ideals of the natural law, eternal and immutable principles of nature which reason discovers and applies. These ideals of reason are believed to be just as universal, absolute and timelessly valid as any ideals of social order and moral good developed by medieval theology. The bourgeois idealists were completely unconscious of the degree to which their own interests and perspectives insinuated themselves into the conception, and even more into the application, of their timeless ideals. Thus liberty assumed a larger significance than either equality or fraternity, because the commercial middle classes were intent upon freeing themselves of the social restraints which a feudal order had placed upon their commercial pursuits. Furthermore urban life was a natural ground of individualism, compared to the more organic social solidarities of agrarian life. The unconscious appropriation of rational ideals for middle-class purposes is most perfectly expressed in John Locke's conviction that the natural law enjoins four rather than three ideals, liberty, equality, fraternity and *property*. It must be added that the unconscious corruption of libertarian ideals, in the early and more idealistic period of bourgeois society, became a conscious corruption in its later and more decadent period, when the struggling merchants and industrialists of the eighteenth century had become the oligarchs of twentieth-century society and conceived liberty to mean the freedom of economic power to express itself without the restraint of government. A comparison of John Stuart Mill's book on Liberty and a more recent volume on the same theme by Herbert Hoover will suggest the trend of this degradation of an ideal. In every Tower of Babel the foundation is more honest than the pinnacle.

Thus the bourgeois world which began by puncturing the illusions and pretensions of the feudal world ends by involving itself in the same illusions.

The "impartial" scientist plays the same spiritual role in it as the medieval priest played in feudal life. Even at this late date this fact is not yet fully apparent to the social scientists of bourgeois ideology. They have yet to learn that the only scientist who can afford to disregard Pilate's cynical sneer "What is truth?" is the physical scientist, and even he may not be competely immune to the temptation of insinuating unexamined presuppositions into his inductions.

Just as the business men discovered the dishonesties of the landed aristocrats, because they had been left out of the alleged paradise of the latter, so the industrial worker assumes the role of rebel and critic in bourgeois society. The industrial worker's most characteristic philosophy is Marxism. The particular virtue of this philosophy is that it brings the Tower of Babel character of all civilisations into the open and makes men conscious of it. It clearly discerns the economic basis of all culture and points a finger of scorn at the claims of impartiality made by the cultural enterprises of the ages. It sees them all as instruments of a social struggle and as rationalisations of interest, as indeed they are. The remarkable characteristic of this philosophy is that, having recognised the finite perspectives of all cultures and the sinful effort to hide and deny this finiteness, it proceeds to construct another Tower of Babel. It proposes to erect

a civilisation in which human finiteness is to be overcome by the perfect balancing of all human interests
in a classless society, thus creating a universal identity
of interest. On the basis of an erroneous identification
of human finiteness with class interests it gives itself
to the false and illusory hope that a classless society
will achieve universal truth. Thus a social class which
sees one aspect of human finiteness and human dishonesty most clearly is tempted to the greatest blindness in regard to the problem of human finiteness
as such. It thus offers a final expression of the perennial pathos of human spirituality: its ability to detect
the spurious claims of impartiality and universality
in every culture except one's own.

The tenth anniversary number of the bulletin of
the League of Fighting Godless in Russia contained
this interesting expression of human pride: "The
Stakhanov movement [which represents a movement
for the organisation of piece work] must play an
outstanding role in the overthrow of religion. It
signifies a mighty increase in the power of man, who
is conquering nature and breaking down all previously
imposed standards. If the scholars of the bourgeois
world maintain that there are limits beyond which
man's perception and man's strength cannot go, that
there are matters which a limited intelligence will
not perceive, it is evident that under the proletarian
deliverance from religion the creation of conscious

workers in a classless society can, with the aid of the latest technical acquisitions, proceed to tasks which man, fettered by religion, would never have dared to face. In a socialist society knowledge is free from narrow limits. Man can learn everything and conquer everything. There is no bulwark which bolshevists cannot take by storm."

There is a curious irony in the fact that bourgeois rationalism wanted to destroy religion because it had built a Tower of Babel while proletarian rationalism seeks to destroy it because it tends to prevent men from building such a tower. Nothing could prove more conclusively that the problem we are considering transcends the boundaries of traditional religion and irreligion. Every form of human culture, whether religious, rational or scientific, is subject to the same corruption, because all are products of the same human heart, which tries to deny its finite limitations. In one sense bourgeois and proletarian criticisms of religion are both right, though they seem to contradict each other. A religious culture always commits the most grievous sin of pretension precisely because it believes in a God who transcends all human knowledge. If it also believes, as it is always tempted to believe, that its own human knowledge can comprehend this transcendence and its human conscience express its imperatives, the Tower of Babel rises just a little higher to its false height.

III

One of the most pathetic aspects of human history is that every civilisation expresses itself most pretentiously, compounds its partial and universal values most convincingly, and claims immortality for its finite existence at the very moment when the decay which leads to death has already begun. Plato projected the peculiar perspectives of the Greek city-state into a universally valid political ideal, partly to arrest the decay of Greek society. In outlining his ideal he seems to have turned from Athens to Sparta for his model, believing the latter to have achieved a higher degree of unity and cohesion. But Spartan unity was the fruit of Spartan militarism; and Spartan militarism, as all militarism, merely arrested social decay at the price of a more inevitable and more sanguinary disintegration.

The Egyptian pyramids were built in a period in which Egyptian civilisation was ripe to the point of overripeness. They expressed the conscious desire of the reigning pharaohs for immortality and the unconscious claim of a whole civilisation to have achieved immortal power. Arnold Toynbee, in his recent *Study of History*, points out that the building of the pyramids accentuated the injustices of the slavery upon which Egyptian civilisation was built, and thus hastened the decay which the pyramids were meant to defy.

The pride of Roman civilisation was Roman law. The final achievement of Roman legalism was the Justinian Code. The Justinian Code was completed in a period when the Roman Empire was already dead, though not yet buried.

Aquinas drew all the strands of medieval culture together in one imposing synthesis. It seemed for the moment as if he had written the outline of a permanent culture and drawn the specifications of a universal civilisation. In it the absolute demands of the Christian gospel were artfully interwoven into the relative necessities of an aristocratic, agrarian society. All this was achieved in the glorious thirteenth century in which the statesmanship of Innocent III and the saintliness of St. Francis illustrated and perfected the practical and the perfectionist sides of Christian thought, so wonderfully synthesised in Thomistic theology. Yet the thirteenth century was not only the greatest but also the last of the medieval centuries. The imposing structure of medievalism cracked in the fourteenth and disintegrated in the fifteenth and sixteenth century. The seed of death was in the very perfection of life of that era.

Perhaps it is too early to seek for similar symbols of doom amidst the most characteristic expressions of our own civilisation. Yet it is significant that the Empire State building in New York, perfect symbol of the pride of a commercial civilisation, was completed just as the great depression came upon us; and it is fairly certain that this great building will never be fully occupied. If such a building expresses the pride and dynamic energy of our civilisation the League of Nations is the characteristic expression of the universalistic dream of bourgeois society. It hoped for eternal peace upon the basis of mutuality of exchange and a rational and prudential adjustment of conflicting national rights and interests. The new League of Nations building in Geneva was completed just in time to hear the Emperor of Abyssinia's vain plea for justice from the League, inability to grant which involved the League in its final ruin.

In every civilisation its most impressive period seems to precede death by only a moment. Like the woods of autumn, life defies death in a glorious pageantry of colour. But the riot of this colour has been distilled by an alchemy in which life has already been touched by death. Thus man claims immortality for his spiritual achievements just when their mortal fate becomes apparent; and death and mortality are strangely mixed into, and potent in, the very pretension of immortality.

IV

We must return to our story to consider one of its most interesting aspects: the form of punishment

41

which a jealous God metes out to those who overleap their mortal state to claim equality with the divine. "And the Lord said—Go to, let us go down, and there confound their language, that they may not understand one another's speech. So the Lord scattered them abroad from thence upon the face of all the earth: and they left off to build the city."

Here we have another mythical profundity which is not literal truth and is yet profoundly true. The peoples of the earth never had one language, unless we regard the babbling of children as a universal language from which the diversity of tongues springs. But it is true that the diversity of languages is a perpetual reminder to proud men that their most perfect temples of the spirit are touched by finiteness. Multiplicity of languages is the most vivid symbol of the fact that the highest pinnacles of the human spirit lie grounded in contingencies of nature and history. Every language is irrational both in comparison with other languages and in terms of its own development. That any language is what it is, that it has this rather than that peculiarity of grammar and syntax, can be understood only if we retrace the history of a whole culture through a thousand vicissitudes.

Languages are the earthern vessels in which the treasures of the spirit are borne. The treasures may, and sometimes do, transcend the limitations of the language. Thus Shakespeare speaks in accents of the heart which may be understood beyond sixteenth-century England; and Cervantes' *Don Quixote* strikes a universal note of tragedy which has relevance beyond the period of dying feudalism, for which his satire was intended; and Goethe sounds notes which will continue to be appreciated beyond the boundaries of German humanism and romanticism. These universal overtones in great literature are reminders of the legitimate pride of the human spirit. Man is not an animal. He is not bound to time or rooted to place. He is

". . . the owner of the spheres,
 Of the seven stars and solar years,
 Of Cæsar's hand and Plato's brain,
 Of the Lord Christ's heart and Shakespeare's strain."

Man touches the fringes of the eternal and universal. Only because he has this dignity can he be tempted to exceed his bounds and claim for the achievements of his spirit a universality which they can never possess. The universal notes in the world's literature are overtones. The multiplicity of languages remains. Cross the border from France to Germany and the sudden change of languages will impress one on occasion as so potent a reality as to be almost physical in its definiteness. These two languages bear imperishable treasures of the human spirit. But they are also freighted with the long sad history of conflict

43

between two European tribes who view each other across a chasm deeper than any chasm of nature; for history accentuates, as well as bridges, the gulfs which nature fixes.

Rationalism is always impatient with these barriers of language and with the irrationality of their divergences. It dreams of a universal language and of a universal culture. But that is merely rationalism's penchant for Towers of Babel; that is the sign of human reason's failure to gauge its own limitations, of its proud and futile defiance of the finite necessities and contingencies which enter into even the proudest edifice of human spirituality.

The Tower of Babel myth is one of the first, as it is one of the most vivid, expressions of the quality of biblical religion. The characteristic distinction of biblical religion, in contrast to culture religions, is that the latter seek to achieve the eternal and divine by some discipline of the mind or heart, whether mystical or rational, while the former believes that a gulf remains fixed between the Creator and the creature which even revelation does not completely bridge. Every revelation of the divine is relativised by the finite mind which comprehends it. Consequently God, though revealed, remains veiled; his thoughts are not our thoughts nor his ways our ways. As high as the heaven is above the earth so high are his thoughts beyond our thoughts and his ways beyond our ways. The worship of such a God leads to contrition; not merely to a contrite recognition of the conscious sins of pride and arrogance which the human spirit commits, but to a sense of guilt for the inevitable and inescapable pride involved in every human enterprise, even in the highest and most perfect or, more correctly, particularly in the highest and noblest human enterprise.

Such a contrition will probably never be perfect enough to save the enterprises of collective man from the periodic catastrophes which overtake them, precisely because they do not know their own limits. But this contrition is possible at least for individuals. Those who understand the limits of human intelligence in the sight of God do not thereby overcome those limits. A man may build a Tower of Babel at the same moment in which he recognises the unjustified pretensions of all human spirituality. It is precisely this conviction, that man faces an inescapable dilemma in the Tower of Babel, which gives the profoundest versions of the Christian religion a supramoral quality. It imparts a sense of contrition not only for moral derelictions but for the unconscious sins involved in the most perfect moral achievements. This is what the Psalmist means when he prays "Enter not into judgment with thy servant, for in thy sight is no man living justified." This is the meaning of the Pauline emphasis upon justification by faith rather than by works. This is the element which modern moralistic Christianity has rejected so completely and for which it has been so gratuitously apologetic. The relevance of this element in Christianity to the ultimate problem of human spirituality has been beyond the ken of modern man, precisely because modern man is a rationalist who builds Towers of Babel without knowing it. The primitive sense of guilt expressed in this myth is the fruit of an insight too profound for modernity's superficial intelligence.

Three:
THE ARK AND
THE TEMPLE

And David assembled all the princes of Israel, the princes of the tribes, and the captains of the companies that ministered to the king by course, and the captains over the thousands, and captains over the hundreds, and the stewards over all the substance and possession of the king, and of his sons, with the officers, and with the mighty men, and with all the valiant men, unto Jerusalem.

Then David the king stood upon his feet, and said, Hear me, my brethren, and my people: As for me, I had in mine heart to build an house of rest for the ark of the covenant of the Lord, and for the footstool of our God, and had made ready the building: But God said unto me, Thou shalt not build an house for my name, because thou hast been a man of war and hast shed blood. Howbeit the Lord God of Israel chose me before all the house of my father to be the king of Israel forever: . . . And he said unto me, Solomon thy son, he shall build my house and my courts: for I have chosen him to be my son, and I will be his father. . . .

Then David gave to Solomon his son the pattern for the porch, and of the houses thereof, and of the treasuries thereof, and of the upper chambers thereof, and of the inner parlours thereof, and of the place of the mercy seat. . . . And David said to Solomon his son, Be strong and of good courage, and do it: fear not, nor be dismayed: for the Lord God, even my God, will be with thee; he will not fail thee, nor forsake thee, until thou hast finished all the work for the service of the house of the Lord. . . . Furthermore David the king said unto all the congregation, Solomon my son, whom alone God hath chosen, is yet young and tender, and the work is great: for the palace is not for man, but for the Lord God. . . .

I Chronicles 28–29:1.

And David said, Blessed be thou, Lord God of Israel our father, forever and ever. Thine, O Lord, is the greatness, and the power, and the glory, and the victory, and the majesty: for all that is in the heaven and in the earth is thine. . . . But who am I, and what is my people, that we should be able to offer so willingly after this sort? for all things come of thee, and of thine own have we given thee. For we are strangers before thee, and sojourners, as were all our fathers: our days on earth are as a shadow, and there is none abiding. . . .

I Chronicles 29:10–15.

Then Solomon began to build the house of the Lord in Jerusalem in mount Moriah, where the Lord appeared unto David his father. . . . Then said Solomon, the Lord hath said that he would dwell in the thick darkness. But I have built an house of habitation for thee, and a place for thy dwelling forever. . . . Now it was in the heart of David my father to build an house for the name of the Lord God of Israel. But the Lord said to David my father, Forasmuch as it was in thine heart to build an house for my name, thou didst well in that it was in thine heart: Notwithstanding thou shalt not build the house; but thy son which shall come forth out of thy loins, he shall build it. . . .

But will God in very deed dwell with men on the earth? behold, heaven and the heaven of heavens cannot contain thee; how much less this house which I have built!

II Chronicles 3:1 and 6:1–18.

3: THE ARK AND THE TEMPLE

I

DAVID was a man of war and also a man of God. He fought to gain ascendancy over the tribes of Israel, uniting them into one kingdom. He also fought to secure the triumph of Israel over surrounding tribes. In all these latter wars the ark of the covenant accompanied him, guaranteeing, as it were, the presence and help of the God of his fathers in his battles. The presence of the ark in all his martial ventures is symbolic of the fact that all men are men of God in their warfare. That distinguishes them from the animals. Men do not fight merely for their existence, though in a sense every human conflict is a primitive contest of life with life. But human life is never mere physical existence. Even the primitive tribe which fights more avowedly and honestly for its existence than modern nations, which always allege devotion to a value higher than their own life, has a racial memory. Therefore the spirits of its dead are with it in present conflict; and, when culture has risen to the height of David's time, the God of the tribe is a companion-in-arms with his people. The ark was the outward symbol of that companionship. Human society, even the most primitive, is more than a contemporary association of people. It is bound to the past and is therefore a sacred brotherhood. Values which transcend its immediate existence are always involved in its conflicts.

The ark of David's religion is a symbol of all culture religion in which the highest values of our devotion are intimately bound up with our own existence. These culture religions always have a god as ambiguous as the God of Israel before the prophets spoke. He is a god who establishes, defends and sanctifies our own values. But he also suggests that these values are not just our own. The gods of primitive society may be frankly tribal gods. But the deities of early civilisation all point to something beyond the tribe. They are the symbols of a profound and disturbing reality in the spiritual life of man. Every high value of human culture has a Janus face. It points to the immediate and to the ultimate. It is a glorification of a particular type of existence, and an effort to transcend the particular and achieve a significance beyond the arbitrary existence out of which it sprang. The gods of culture religion are therefore always gods of battle, who help gain victory in the battle because they are a little more than gods of battle. The *Pax Romana* was thus a Roman peace, based on Roman arms. But it was more than a Roman peace in that it was a peace from which even the subjects and victims of Rome secured a benefit. The principle of social peace transcended Roman power. The God of bourgeois society is more than bourgeois society. He is the god of liberty, democracy and fraternity. But he is also the god of battles. Every one of these universal values is involved in the necessities of bourgeois existence and is in conflict with other equally worthy values.

The god of American religion (the so-called "American dream") is an American god; yet he is god and not just America, because the freedom of opportunity which America offered the class-ridden peoples of Europe, when America was at her best, was a human and not just an American value. The god of feudal Europe, even when he was supposedly the God of Christian faith, was a god of battles. He was the god of a particular type of agrarian civilisation and of a unique medieval culture. In Spain they are still doing battle for him; and they call their war a war for "Christian civilisation."

The god of a culture and a civilisation is thus always the god of the ark which accompanies the warrior. He is the god of a particular culture in conflict with other cultures; the god of a particular type of human existence in conflict with other types of human life. Yet he is more than that; and it is by that *more* that he becomes an effective ally in the battle. For human beings who develop a life which involves more than existence do not fight well if they are not certain that more than existence is involved in the struggle. The god of the ark is thus the source of what in modern days is called "morale."

II

If religion were no more than this culture religion (and it frequently is no more than that even in a Christian age), we should be forced to admit the essential polytheism of all religious life. The gods of the ark make warfare more terrible in that they endow each contestant with the certainty of fighting for something greater than himself; a certainty which leads to righteous fury and cruelty. But the very ambiguity of the god of the ark which creates this fury also points beyond itself. This is the inchoate monotheism which is involved in all advanced polytheism. Perhaps the best symbol of it is the fact that the god of a particular nation is usually also the creator of the world. That is, he is really the author of all of life and is therefore not bound to the nation. It was the achievement and the glory of the Hebrew Prophets to develop this pure monotheism fully.

David (or at least the priestly writers who interpreted David's spiritual life) agreed with the prophets. When David, the man of war, stopped fighting, and decided to build a temple to house the ark in place of the itinerant tabernacle of the battlefield, the same God who had given victory in battle now seemed to change His character. He stayed David's hand. David was not good enough to build a temple to God. "Thou hast shed blood." David was too deeply involved in the conflict of life with life. The God who spoke to David in that hour was a god who transcended the partial and relative values which are in conflict in all historical struggles. It was the same God who spoke through the mouth of Amos, "Are ye not as the children of the Ethiopians unto me?"

In fact, his voice was so different and his counsels so divergent that one may ask the question whether this was not an altogether different God from the god of the ark. "It is clear," writes Julien Benda, "that there are two gods and that they have nothing to do with each other. The God whom Marshal de Villars rising in his stirrups and pointing his sword to the skies thanks on the evening of Demain, is not the same God in whose bosom Thomas à Kempis learns the nothingness of all human victories." This God who spoke through David's uneasy conscience is the God of the prophets and of Christ. He is the God about whom Jesus said: "Why callest thou me good? none is good, save one, that is God." This is the God "who bringeth the princes to naught and maketh the judges of the world as vanity." This is the God before whom the nations are as "a drop in the bucket." This God is not the ally of the nations but their judge and their redeemer. He is not the sanctity of our highest values, but the Holiness before whom "all our righteousnesses are as filthy rags." Whether there is any relation between this God and the sanctities of the ark is a question we will postpone for the moment, while we analyse David's problem.

David's problem was: How can a man involved in the conflicts of life build a temple to a God who transcends those conflicts and who judges the sins involved in our highest values? Various solutions to this problem are offered in this remarkable text. The first and most obvious solution is the least satisfactory. It is a moral solution which is not without a certain pathos and beauty. Said David: I am not good enough to build the temple, but "my son is young and tender." Let the temple be built by the purity of youth. It has not yet involved itself in the conflicts of life. Let it be built by a stable rather than a warring civilisation. This is a moral solution. It seeks to find some one good enough to build the temple of God. In terms of a modern analogy it is the sectarian solution. The sectarian church usually protests that the members of the orthodox church are not worthy to belong to it. The sect therefore builds a new church with wholly regenerate members. The sectarian traditions of American Protestantism incline the American church on the whole to this solution. The church conceives of itself as a body of people who are seeking to live by the law of Christ and the will of God and thus try to make themselves worthy to build the church.

The symbol of the error of this solution in this ancient chronicle is a perfect one. Solomon did indeed build the temple. But was he really better than David? He may have been "young and tender" but he was not so tender when he was no longer so young. His reign may have been less warlike than David's; but its stability rested upon David's triumphs. Furthermore the stability was marred by injustice. Did not the rebels under Jeroboam come to Rehoboam, Solomon's son, with the indictment "Your father's yoke was grievous"? To say nothing of the pride with which Solomon sought to impress the Queen of Sheba, his reign paid a heavy price for the munificence of its stability. The price was vexatious taxation. One has the uneasy feeling that the very building of the temple may have added to the tax burden. Stable and peaceful societies usually have a higher culture than more primitive and warlike communities. But there is a disquieting relation between culture and injustice from Solomon's day to our own. Solomon's extravagant building programme belongs to the same category of culture as the grand opera of our metropolitan centres, in which a great art is supported primarily by the proud plutocrats who sit in the "diamond horseshoe." No one can estimate what the monetary power, by which these enterprises are supported, has cost the poor. Even institutions of culture which are less obviously the toys and playthings of the rich, universities for instance, have a disquieting relation to economic injustice. Their endowments have been gathered from the crumbs which have fallen from Dives' table.

No civilisation has yet solved the problem of the too intimate relation between culture and social injustice. The great civilisations of Egypt, Babylon and Rome were all superior to primitive society in the extent of their social stability and the elaboration of their culture; but they were all inferior to primitive society in the character of their social justice. Moreover, their peace rested upon the sword no less than the anarchy of primitive society was created by the sword.

The dubious character of Solomon's superiority over David contains a particular lesson for America. It achieved dominion over a whole continent with comparatively little effort and is consequently inclined to forget that an imperial impulse prompted the conquest of Oregon, California and Texas. It is a Solomonic civilisation which denies or forgets that it ever had a David preceding Solomon. Whether it makes that mistake or not, its national life is constantly tempted to self-righteous pride in comparing itself with the warring nations of Europe. It feels itself immeasurably superior to the civilisations in which the contest of power and the conflict of life have been more obvious. Yet the civilisations in which conflict is overt rather than covert are usually less self-deceived, just as David's conscience was more sensitive than Solomon's.

The lesson is obvious for the whole Anglo-Saxon world as well as for America. The Anglo-Saxon nations are inclined to be pharisaic in judging the more warlike nations of the continent, just as privileged groups in every nation are morally censorious toward the underprivileged groups who threaten to destroy the "law and order" of the *status quo*. They forget to what degree pacifism may be a luxury of nations and classes who have what they want, and who defend their privileges in the name of peace rather than seek new advantages by war. There is a pacifism which seeks, by honest religious discipline, to transcend the conflicts of history and to make itself worthy of the temple of God. But such pure religious pacifism is comparatively rare; and even it is parasitic upon the power by which David has stabilised the civilisation in which it exists.

There is, in short, no method by which men can extricate themselves so completely from the warfare of human existence as to be worthy of building a temple dedicated to the God in whose bosom we learn "the nothingness of all human victories." There is no way of moral striving to build the church of God.

III

The real fact is that the temple of God was built not by Solomon's goodness but by David's uneasy conscience. The church is created not by the righteousness of the pharisee but the contrition of the publican; not by the achievement of pure goodness but by the recognition of the sinfulness of all human goodness. This contrition is the fruit of faith in the transcendent God who cannot be identified with any human goodness. The prayer attributed to David expresses faith in this God beautifully: "Thine is the majesty and the power and the victory; we are but sojourners and strangers—we are as a shadow that declineth." Here is the recognition of human creatureliness before God and the "vanity of all human victories," which must enter into the life of any church which is more than the sanctification of human ideals. Even Solomon has some recognition of the true church in the prayer with which he dedicates the temple: "The heavens cannot contain thee, how much less this house which I have built." The church is not a congregation of people who can pride themselves upon their unique goodness. It is rather a congregation of people to whom the eternal God has spoken and who answer the eternal word in terms of Job's contrition: "I have uttered things too wonderful for me, which I understood not. Wherefore I abhor myself and repent in dust and ashes."

Man's contrition is the human foundation of the church. But God's grace is its completion. The God who denied David the right to build the temple had a remarkable word of consolation for him: "Since it was in thine heart [to build the temple] thou dost well that it was in thine heart." Man is a creature of time and place and all of his ideals are coloured by the interests which spring from his temporal existence. He follows the ark of his own ideals. Yet the eternal God speaks to him and he would feign build a temple which transcends the ark. He sees the possibility of a truth which is more than his truth and of a goodness which is more than his goodness. He contemplates the eternal but he cannot name it. When he names it he gives it a name which introduces, again, his own finite perspectives. He cannot even worship the Christ without drawing images of him which make it appear that Christ is his own peculiar possession. Ignatius Loyola was a warrior and a monk, and his Christ was a combination of a warrior and a monk. Francis of Assisi was a pure ascetic and his Christ was a pure monk. Gregory VII was a Cæsar and a pope, and his Christ was half Cæsar and half pope. Yet insofar as each of these men had something of the eternal vision he was also disturbed by the disquieting sense that Christ was more than his particular good.

The church is that place in human society where men are disturbed by the word of the eternal God, which stands as a judgment upon human aspirations. But it is also the place where the word of mercy, reconciliation and consolation is heard: "Thou dost well that it was in thine heart." Here human incompleteness is transcended though not abolished. Here human sin is overcome by the divine mercy, though man remains a sinner. No church can lift man out of the partial and finite history in which all human life stands. Every interpretation of the church which promises an "efficient grace," by which man ceases to be man and enters prematurely into the Kingdom of God, is a snare and a delusion. The church is not the Kingdom of God. The Church is the place in human society where the Kingdom of God impinges upon all human enterprises through the divine word, and where the grace of God is made available to those who have accepted His judgment.

IV

One further significant fact remains to be recorded in regard to the temple and the ark. The ark was placed in the temple. The symbol of the god of battles found a resting place in the temple dedicated to the God of peace who condemned David's shedding of blood. The god of the ark who both transcended and sanctified the highest sanctities of Israel was subordinated to the God of the temple, but not wholly excluded from its worship. The prophets were more rigorous than that. For the prophets the gods of particular nations were demons. The eternal God stood against these gods. But in the temple the ark found a resting place. The difference is one between priestly and prophetic religion. Prophetic religion is more rigorous than priestly religion. It speaks an eternal "no" to all human pretensions. Priestly religion, on the other hand, appreciates what points to the eternal in all human values. The priest is the poet who comprehends the meaning of human activities in the light of the eternal purpose. For him they do not deny but partially fulfil the will of God. The priest does not say, "whoso loveth father and mother more than me is not worthy of me." Rather he gives family life a sacramental character. He sees the love which is achieved between members of the family as a sign and token of a more perfect love. In that sense Jesus was priest as well as prophet when he said, "If ye then being evil know how to give good gifts unto your children, how much more shall your Father which is in heaven give good things to them that ask him." That is, the imperfect human achievement is a symbol and sacrament of the eternal.

The priest does not condemn a man's love for his country, though there is always the possibility that the nation will usurp the place of God and make itself the center and source of all meaning. The priest sees in men's devotion to a cause greater than themselves the possibility of faith and devotion to the God who is greater than the causes which are greater than man.

There is no way of arriving at a perfect compromise between the priest and the prophet, between the faith which incorporates the ark into the temple and that which regards the god of the ark as the devil. The ambiguous character of all human spirituality makes this impossible. On the whole the religion of the priest is more dangerous than that of the prophet. He places the ark in the temple and tempts men to regard the god of the ark as the eternal God. They will be the more inclined to do this, as the ark is in the temple, and the aura of the temple and its vast dimensions seem to enhance the proportions of the ark. Thus the Christian church, despite its ostensible devotion to the eternal God, is most frequently a temple with an ark. The national flags which hang in the sanctuary are symbols of this fact. But even if the symbol be lacking, the ark is there in reality. Many a church is more devoted to the characteristic ideals of its national life than to the Kingdom of God in the light of which these ideals are seen in their pettiness and sinfulness. For this reason the word of the prophet must always be heard. The prophet is an iconoclast who throws all symbols of human goodness out of the temple. Only the word of the eternal God must be heard in the temple, a word of judgment upon human sin and of mercy for sinners.

But the unambiguous word of the prophet may do injustice to the ambiguity of the human enterprise. That ambiguity may be the source of dishonesty and pretension. But it is also the source of all genuine creativity in human history. The god of the ark is never purely the devil. Human goodness is never merely pretension. Its reaching beyond itself is at once the root of its sin and the proof of man's destiny as a child of God. Man stands under and in eternity. His imagination is quickened by the vision of an eternal good. Following that vision, he is constantly involved both in the sin of giving a spurious sanctity to his imperfect good and in the genuine creativity of seeking a higher good than he possesses.

Whatever the prophets may say therefore, there will always be King Davids. Nor could history exist without them. They are actually the authors of all human enterprise. Many of them do not have David's uneasy conscience. Their religion never transcends devotion to the ark. But even those who hear the word of the Eternal and in moments of high insight

65

confess "we are but sojourners and strangers—we are
as a shadow that declineth" cannot for that reason
cease from performing the tasks of to-day and to-
morrow.

It is significant that America, for all of its simple
religion of the ark, had at least one statesman,
Abraham Lincoln, who understood exactly what
David experienced. Lincoln was devoted both to
the Union and to the cause of the abolition of slavery,
though he subordinated the latter to the former.
Speaking of the divergent ideals of the north and
south he said, "Both read the same Bible and pray
to the same God, and each invokes his aid against
the other. The prayers of both could not be answered." Here is the recognition of the will of God
which transcends the northern and the southern
idealism. Stephen Vincent Benét puts this insight of
Lincoln in the memorable words:

"They come to me and talk about God's will
  In righteous deputations and platoons,
  Day after day, laymen and ministers.
  They write me Prayers From Twenty Million Souls
  Defining me God's will and Horace Greeley's.
  God's will is General This and Senator That,
  God's will is those poor coloured fellows' will,
  It is the will of the Chicago churches,
  It is this man's and his worst enemy's.
  But all of them are sure they know God's will.
  I am the only man who does not know it."

"And, yet, if it is probable that God
  Should, and so very clearly, state his will
  To others, on a point of my own duty,
  It might be thought He would reveal it me
  Directly, more especially as I
  So earnestly desire to know His will."[1]

Yet this religious insight into the inscrutability of the divine does not deter Lincoln from making moral judgments according to his best insight. He continues in his Second Inaugural: "It may seem strange that men should ask the assistance of a just God in wringing their bread from other men's toil." That is a purely moral judgment and a necessary one. That is devotion to the highest moral ideal we know, which in this case was the ideal of freedom for all men. But Lincoln returns immediately to the other level: "But let us judge not that we be not judged." One could scarcely find a better example of a consummate interweaving of moral idealism and a religious recognition of the imperfection of all human ideals. It is out of such a moral and religious life that the moving generosity is born which Lincoln expressed in the words, "With malice toward none, with charity toward all, let us strive to finish the work we are in." This is a religion in which the ark has not been removed from the temple, but in which the temple is more than the ark. Unfortunately the Christian

[1] From *John Brown's Body*, p. 213. Published by Farrar and Rinehart, Inc. Copyright, 1927, 1928, by Stephen Vincent Benét.

Church manages only occasionally to relate the ark to the temple as perfectly as that. But the example of Lincoln, as well as of David, reveals the possibility.

Four:
FOUR HUNDRED
TO ONE

And it came to pass in the third year, that Jehoshaphat, the king of Judah came down to the king of Israel. And the king of Israel said unto his servants, Know ye that Ramoth in Gilead is ours and we be still, and take it not out of the hand of the king of Syria?

And he said unto Jehoshaphat, Wilt thou go with me to battle to Ramoth-gilead? And Jehoshaphat said to the king of Israel, I am as thou art, my people as thy people, my horses as thy horses. And Jehoshaphat said unto the king of Israel, Enquire, I pray thee, at the word of the Lord today.

Then the king of Israel gathered the prophets together, about four hundred men, and said unto them, Shall I go against Ramoth-gilead to battle or shall I forbear? And they said, Go up; for the Lord shall deliver it into the hand of the king.

And Jehoshaphat said, Is there not here a prophet of the Lord besides that we might enquire of him? And the king of Israel said unto Jehoshaphat, There is yet one man, Micaiah the son of Imlah, by whom we may enquire of the Lord: but I hate him; for he doth not prophesy good concerning me, but evil. And Jehoshaphat said, Let not the king say so.

Then the king of Israel called an officer and said, Hasten hither Micaiah the son of Imlah. And the king of Israel and Jehoshaphat the king of Judah sat each on his throne, having put on their robes, in a void place in the entrance of the gate of Samaria; and all the prophets prophesied before them. And Zedekiah the son of Chenaanah made him horns of iron: and he said, Thus saith the Lord, With these shalt thou push the Syrians, until thou have consumed them. And all the prophets prophesied so, saying, Go up to Ramoth-

gilead, and prosper: for the Lord shall deliver it into the king's hand.

And the messenger that was gone to call Micaiah spake unto him, saying, Behold now, the words of the prophets declare good unto the king with one mouth: let thy word, I pray thee, be like the word of one of them, and speak that which is good. And Micaiah said, As the Lord liveth, what the Lord saith unto me, that will I speak.

So he came to the king. And the king said unto him, Micaiah, shall we go against Ramoth-gilead to battle or shall we forbear? And he answered him, Go, and prosper: for the Lord shall deliver it into the hand of the king. And the king said unto him, How many times shall I adjure thee that thou tell me nothing but that which is true in the name of the Lord? And he said, I saw all Israel scattered upon the hills, as sheep that have not a shepherd: and the Lord said, These have no master, let them return every man to his home in peace.

And the king of Israel said unto Jehoshaphat, Did I not tell thee that he would prophesy no good concerning me, but evil? And he said, Hear thou therefore the word of the Lord: I saw the Lord sitting on his throne, and all the host of heaven standing by him on his right hand and on his left. And the Lord said, Who shall persuade Ahab that he may go up and fall at Ramoth-gilead? And one said on this manner, and another said on that manner. And there came forth a spirit, and stood before the Lord, and said, I will persuade him. And the Lord said unto him, Wherewith? And he said, I will go forth, and I will be a lying spirit in the mouth of all his prophets. And he said, thou shalt per-suade him, and prevail also: go forth and do so. . . .

And the king of Israel said, Take Micaiah, and carry him back unto Amon the governor of the city, and to Joash the king's son; And say, Thus saith the king, Put this fellow in the prison and feed him with the bread of affliction and with water of affliction, until I come in peace. And Micaiah said, If thou return at all in peace, the Lord hath not spoken by me.

I Kings 22:2–28.

4: FOUR HUNDRED
TO ONE

THE most primitive religion is magic; and magic is a kind of crude science which seeks to bend natural and cosmic forces to the human will. Even when magic has been supplanted by tribal polytheism, religion remains an effort to glorify and to assure the success of the cause closest to the devotee's heart. Yet there is in even the most primitive religion a suggestion of a higher purpose. This purpose is to bend the human will to the divine will, to discover the ultimate truth about life to which men ought to submit, whatever their inclinations. These two contrasting motives in religion are always at war and never achieve a stable equilibrium. The lowest religion is never purely an effort to bend the world to human wishes: and the highest religion, in actual practice, mixes motives of self-glorification into the honest purpose of subjecting the individual will to the purposes of God.

I

Consider this vivid story of the kings of Israel and of Judah. The king of Israel wanted to go to

73

war and desired the help of the king of Judah. The king of Judah was willing to join forces with Ahab; but he desired a divine oracle to allay lurking doubts about the enterprise. "Enquire I pray thee," said he, "at the word of the Lord this day." It is not immediately apparent whether the king of Judah was primarily interested in the rightness of war or in its probable success. But it soon becomes apparent that he thought of the "word of the Lord" as a disinterested judgment which was not dictated by the interests of his royal ally. The king of Israel had a more cynical attitude toward religion. You want some divine assurance for this battle, said he in effect. I will be glad to give it to you. I have four hundred prophets attached to my court and I will summon them immediately.

The four hundred prophets, soothsayers, magicians and priests were summoned. The king asked them whether he should go to war against Ramoth-gilead; and the prophets assured him that he should and that success would crown his efforts: "The Lord will deliver Ramoth-gilead into the hand of the king." The king of Israel was not satisfied with this performance. The very unanimity of the prophetic verdict on the martial enterprise sowed seeds of suspicion in his mind. It is not frequently that four hundred prophets, wise men, preachers, academicians or seers speak with one voice. In this case the king of Judah probably

suspected that the man who paid the piper had called
the tune. After all, the prophets were attached to the
court of the king of Israel. As many prophets thus
attached before and since, they were no more reliable
than the king's courtiers. There have been periods
of history in which the king's jester was a truer
prophet than the king's chaplain. Perhaps the king
of Judah was specially aroused by Zedekiah, the son
of Chanaanah, a particularly sensational prophet, who
ran up and down before the thrones with two horns
of iron to give a vivid illustration of the prospective
victory of the two kings. Zedekiah was perhaps the
first pulpit sensationalist engaged in the dubious
practice of echoing popular prejudices and adding
nothing to them but an excess of emotion.

The king of Judah betrayed his suspicions by the
simple request: "Is there not a prophet of the Lord
beside that we might enquire of him?" In other words:
Could you not produce a more authentic prophet?
Yes, said the king of Israel, there is another but I
hate him. He never prophesies good concerning me
but evil. The king of Israel probably did not realise
what a splendid recommendation for Micaiah's
authenticity this accusation was. But it was not lost on
the king of Judah. "Let not the king say so," he
answered, which we may interpret as meaning: perhaps this prophet is merely trying to tell the truth.

At any rate, the king of Israel was too anxious for

the support of Jehoshaphat to risk offending him. Therefore he sent for Micaiah. The messenger of the king, who brought Micaiah, was a perfect diplomat. What he said to Micaiah in effect was: The two kings are on their thrones at the gate of Samaria trying to decide whether to go to war. They have asked all the men of God and they have with one voice advised such a course. Now if it is not inconsistent with your general principles, we hope you will maintain the unanimity of the verdict. We may pause to observe that the king's messengers usually speak in terms equally suave to the prophets of every age; and false or simple prophets are generally greatly impressed by the king's kind and gentle words. The church is bent to the uses of men of power by just this kind of diplomacy. When Henry VIII declared himself spiritual ruler over the Church of England he used exactly the same argument, used by Ahab's messenger, upon the recalcitrant Thomas More. More had served the king long and faithfully as his chancellor. But he was not willing to subject the Church of God to secular authority. The king argued that since every one in the church had agreed to the plan, More was guilty of irresponsible caprice in offering solitary opposition. Yet the word of the Lord has frequently been spoken most authentically by a solitary prophet, whose word defied both king and prophets.

Micaiah gave some indication of his mettle by his answer to the king's messenger: "As the Lord liveth, what the Lord saith unto me, that will I speak." Here was a prophet, long before the great eighth-century prophets, who understood how to meet the dangers of corruption in prophecy and who dared to defy the king in the name of the word which God had given him to speak. These early prophets, who ate the king's bread and humoured the king's whims, were a motley and undignified crowd. That a Micaiah should have been among them and that he should have perceived so clearly his duty toward a higher authority than the king is an interesting example of the eruption of pure religion in the domain of servile religion. Micaiah's word to the king's messenger explains the king's previous statement: "There is yet another prophet, but I hate him, for he doth not prophesy good concerning me but evil."

When Micaiah finally stood before the two kings and the question of the war against Ramoth-gilead was posed, he took the king of Israel by surprise in seeming to agree with the word of the other prophets. He sanctioned the war and prophesied triumph for the king's cause. The king was taken aback by this acquiescence and said: "How many times shall I adjure thee to tell me nothing but that which is true in the name of the Lord?" You know then, said Micaiah in effect, that I am not telling you the truth and that these other prophets are lying. You have proposed a certain action and wanted to use the prophets merely to reinforce your own will. Yet you have an uneasy conscience and it is not reassured by lying prophets who have so frequently agreed with you before. Whereupon Micaiah painted a dire picture of the disaster which would befall Israel through the proposed war. The consequence of this defiance was Micaiah's banishment to prison, where many a true prophet has been consigned before and since.

II

So runs this vivid story of early prophecy and its perils. In analysing it we may profitably begin with a comparison of the two kings who consulted the men of God, in order to know the "word of the Lord." It would not be quite accurate to make the king of Judah the symbol and example of the human desire to submit our will to the divine, and the king of Israel the symbol of the constant temptation to harness the ultimate to our immediate purposes. Yet there was a difference between the two kings. Perhaps both forces of religion were at war in the soul of each, as they are in all of us; but in the king of Israel the utilitarian use of religion was his dominant interest, while in the king of Judah a higher degree of honesty was evident.

Both kings reveal a curious compound of religious

interests. The king of Israel wanted the prophets to justify what he intended to do. Yet even he could not be satisfied completely with prophets who were too certain to conform their judgments to his whim and will. A religion which seeks to bend cosmic forces to the human will at least admits that there are forces which are not immediately under the control of the human will. And a religion which seeks to justify immediate purposes by ultimate ones concedes by implication that immediate purposes cannot justify themselves. They must be proved to be in some harmonious relation to the ultimate. No cultural force, whether science, religion or philosophy can ever be the prostitute of a particular cause, if it is only that. A prophet who speaks only what the king wants to hear ceases ere long to be of use even to the king. This is a fact which the Marxian theory of ideology does not always comprehend. Counterfeit money is impossible if there is not some real money; and counterfeit culture is self-defeating if there is not a core of honesty in the cultural enterprise.

Men are always trying to prove that what they are doing is in accord with God's will or with ultimate truth or with the supreme good. But they can do this only on the supposition that there is a will beyond their own, a truth higher than their knowledge and a good better than their own. Thus even a religion which is primarily the servant of human purposes points beyond itself. There is a touching story of Henry VIII's pathetic anxiety to convince the great humanist Colet of the justice of one of his martial ventures. Henry had many courtiers and ecclesiasts about him who were ready enough to ease his conscience on any cause he cared to undertake. But their very servility made them ineffective. Therefore Henry sought to persuade an honest man that his cause was just. Henry's relation to Colet and More bears striking similarities to Ahab's relation to Micaiah.

If the king of Judah was a little more sceptical of the testimony of unanimous prophets, that also reveals a conflict of religious forces in his soul. He may have been innately more honest than the king of Israel. On the other hand, it must be remembered that the prophets whose honesty he suspected were not his own but Ahab's. Perhaps that was the real cause of his scepticism. It is always easier to puncture the pretensions of others than our own hypocrisies. That is what imparts such a peculiar pathos to the relationship of nations. Each nation sees the hypocrisies of its neighbours with cynical penetration: but it usually makes hypocritical pretensions of its own in the same breath. The reason each nation is so certain that it possesses a higher degree of honesty than its neighbours is that what appears as hypocrisy from the outside is usually only self-deception from the inside. We fool our neighbours because we have first fooled ourselves. And there is always a religious quality in this self-deception. We want our will to prevail; yet we know that it cannot prevail if it conflicts with the eternal order of the world. Therefore we seek in the same act and the same thought to conform our will to God's and to coerce God's will to our own. This curious deception may be detected by others but not by ourselves. Yet the others, who detect it, erroneously imagine themselves our moral superiors. The king of Judah may therefore have been no more honest than the king of Israel.

III

The purity of the word of God depends upon Micaiah rather than upon the king of Judah. In other words the religious desires and ambitions of all men are too mixed to permit us to make absolutely just distinctions between pure and impure religion. Yet we know that the word of God has been spoken to men honestly, even when they were not certain that they wanted to hear it in its purity.

Micaiah was an obscure prophet and we know nothing about the sources and the criteria of his "word of the Lord" but what is revealed in this story. We do not therefore gain a clear knowledge of his prophetic depth. Yet two facts stand out clearly. One is that there was, even in this early tribal religion, an occasional apprehension of the profound religious truth that God is not simply the sum total of the highest social values, and that therefore the word of God must frequently be spoken against the community and king, and not for them. It was this insight which the later eighth-century prophets elaborated, so that their religion ceased to be the religion of a tribe and became the revelation of the will of a transcendent God, spoken to and against all nations. We do not know whether Micaiah had any adequate test for distinguishing between the ultimate word of God and human prejudices. Perhaps he did not have. We only know that he honestly believed in such a word and felt himself in possession of it. Micaiah's prophetic ministry is therefore proof of the inadequacy of purely social interpretations of religion, such as those of Durkheim and Levy-Bruhl. The religion of early civilisations is little more than a glorification and sanctification of tribal and national purposes. Yet there were priests and prophets in both the great empires of Egypt and Babylon who felt under compulsion to criticise rather than to sanctify the aspirations of the community and the ambitions of the king. They expressed, as Micaiah did, the overtone of pure transcendence which is to be found in even tribal and social religion.

It must be admitted that Micaiah was only one prophet among four hundred. Perhaps the percentage

of pure prophecy to false prophecy is not much higher
even today, though the Christian Church has a revelation of the God and Father of our Lord Jesus Christ,
who obviously is not the God of any particular nation
and cannot be made the ally of any particular cause.
Nevertheless the force of natural religion against the
truth of this revelation remains powerful, and dominates not only many churches but many ministers of
the word. Only the most rigorous searching of hearts
can prevent prophets from mixing the prejudices of
communities and the desires of kings with the counsels of God, and offering the compound as the word
of the Lord.

The second interesting fact about Micaiah is that
it required courage to speak the word of the Lord
against the king. Courage is still one of the tests of
true prophecy. Not all prophets are put in prison: but
there are times when all of them are threatened with
punishment. The world is composed of communities
so large as to imagine themselves the ultimate community but not large enough to deserve being regarded as custodians of ultimate values. The pride
and pretensions of these communities is a constant
hazard to true prophecy. Sometimes the king is
merely a symbol of such a community and articulates
its pride. Sometimes the king has his own pride,
which he seeks to glorify at the expense of the community. In either case there is a constant pressure

upon the church and the preachers of the word to conform their message to the needs, the prejudices and the desires of the community and its leaders. Against such pressure the prophet can set no force but his own courage.

Some nations imagine that the problem of the relation of church and state has been solved by the conception of a free church in a free state. But no particular formula can solve this problem. The absence of conflict between church and state in America, for instance, is due primarily not to this formula but to the fact that neither state nor church has been fully developed or defined in a great, amorphous and not yet highly articulated community. But meanwhile the American state is developing and increasing its powers and the church must gradually recognise that it is something more than the community at prayer. The church is the body of Christ: and Christ is the revelation of the living God, the creator, judge and redeemer of all nations. Such a fellowship can never be completely at home in any nation or perfectly conform to national purposes and ambitions. The conflict between Christianity and the state will become particularly apparent in times of war; but it will not be perfectly understood if it is not anticipated in other than martial periods. In every community, whether ostensibly Christian or not, there is an innate and inherent tendency toward self-glorification. Nowhere is the temptation to idolatry greater than in national life. The nation is so much larger than the individual that it not only naturally claims to be the individual's god but naturally impresses the individual with the legitimacy of this claim.

This national idolatry has become a particularly virulent form of sin in the contemporary period. There is no place in the world to-day in which the church must not contend against it. In some nations the issue is definitely joined. In them the word of God is actually spoken with greater clarity than where the issue is not joined. In America, for instance, there are still many prophets of God who imagine that Christianity and the religion "of the American dream" are one and the same thing. These prophets imagine that "democracy is the social and political expression of Christianity," and that a nation which has abolished kings has also overcome the pride of nations. They do not know what a proud, vexatious and cruel king Demos may become on occasion.

To speak the word of God against king Demos therefore requires not only courage but penetration. Illusions must be dispelled. Yet courage remains a primary test of prophecy. There is no national community to-day in which a genuine word of God does not place the prophet in peril. The kings of modern communities are most frequently financial and industrial oligarchs who make war against Ramoth-gilead in a series of social conflicts. Ramoth-gilead is usually a labour union. They have the same motley crew of prophets in their court which Ahab boasted, servile priests of religion who wail about an imperilled "law and order." On the other hand, the same labour movement which fights for basic justice in capitalistic countries may, when as in Russia it achieves victory, express itself in an idolatrous pride and spawn as vexatious and arrogant oligarchs as any community. The servile priests of Russia to-day are the teachers of the schools who persuade their children to write ridiculous letters to Stalin, thanking him for the murder of "traitors."

There is no conceivable society in which the pride of the community and the arrogance of its oligarchs must not be resisted. It is possible to offer this resistance at times in the name of some minority interest. But the final resistance must come from the community which knows and worships a God, to whom all nations are subject. Sometimes the testimony of the prophet of this God speaks in a common voice with the criticisms of political minorities; it may on occasion be very necessary and important that the two types of defiance be joined. Yet they are never one and the same thing. The Christian Church must be and remain a fellowship of Christ; and

Christ is the judge of the self-will and self-righteousness of every social group.

Against the temptations to cowardice and conformity the heroic story of Micaiah is a constant source of courage and inspiration. The history of the Christian Church is replete with the embarrassing submissions of prophets and priests to the pride and arrogance of nations and rulers. Yet, as long as any spark of prophecy remains within, it will have, as it has had, Micaiahs who will know how to say, "As the Lord liveth, what the Lord saith unto me, that will I speak."

Five:
THE TEST OF
TRUE PROPHECY

Woe be unto the pastors that destroy and scatter the sheep of my pasture! saith the Lord. Therefore thus saith the Lord God of Israel against the pastors that feed my people; Ye have scattered my flock, and driven them away, and have not visited them: behold, I will visit upon you the evil of your doings, saith the Lord. And I will gather the remnant of my flock out of all countries whither I have driven them, and will bring them again to their folds; and they shall be fruitful and increase. And I will set up shepherds over them which shall feed them: and they shall fear no more, nor be dismayed, neither shall they be lacking, saith the Lord. . . .

Mine heart within me is broken because of the prophets; all my bones shake; I am like a drunken man, and like a man whom wine hath overcome, because of the Lord, and because of the words of his holiness. . . .

Thus saith the Lord of hosts, Hearken not unto the words of the prophets that prophesy unto you: they make you vain: they speak a vision of their own heart, and not out of the mouth of the Lord. They say still unto them that despise me, The Lord hath said, Ye shall have peace; and they say unto every one that walketh after the imagination of his own heart, No evil shall come upon you. *For who hath stood in the counsel of the Lord, and hath perceived and heard his word? who hath marked his word and heard it?*

Behold, a whirlwind of the Lord is gone forth in fury, even a grievous whirlwind: it shall fall grievously upon the head of the wicked. The anger of the Lord shall not return, until he have executed, and till he have performed the thoughts of his heart: in the latter days ye shall consider it perfectly. I have not sent these prophets, yet they ran: I have not spoken to them, yet they prophesied. But if they had stood in my counsel, and had caused my people to hear my words, then they should have turned them from their evil way, and from the evil of their doings. . . .

The prophet that hath a dream, let him tell a dream; and he that hath my word, let him speak my word, faithfully. What is the chaff to the wheat? saith the Lord. Is not my word like as a fire? saith the Lord; and like a hammer that breaketh the rock in pieces? Therefore, behold, I am against the prophets, saith the Lord, that steal my words every one from his neighbour. Behold, I am against the prophets, saith the Lord, that use their tongues, and say, He saith. Behold, I am against them that prophesy false dreams, saith the Lord, and do tell them, and cause my people to err by their lies, and by their lightness; yet I sent them not, nor commanded them: therefore they shall not profit this people at all, saith the Lord.

Jeremiah 23:1–32.

5: THE TEST OF
TRUE PROPHECY

WHEN a man speaks in the name
of God and prefixes his pronouncements with a "Thus
saith the Lord," he is either a fool, or a knave or—a
prophet. How is one to know into which category he
belongs? How is one to judge the eternal word and
to know when the prejudice of an hour or the foolish
opinion of a man has been falsely arrayed in the
pretense of divine wisdom? The history of religion
is full of the chronicles of both fools and knaves and
our insane asylums still boast their due quotas of
unhappy maniacs who think they are messiahs. By
what criterion is one to discover what is true and
what is false in the conflicting claims of competing
messiahs and prophets?

The prophet Jeremiah is very much concerned
with the problem of false prophets. He deals with
it repeatedly. The test he presents for distinguishing
between the true and false in prophecy may not be
exhaustive. The problem is too great to be easily
exhausted. But his test is important and convincing.
Jeremiah accuses some of the prophets of his day of

93

speaking "the vision of their own heart and not out of the mouth of the Lord." But that is merely to describe false prophecy. False prophecy always means to give ultimate significance to purely individual and partial judgments. The question is: How is one to detect this false element? Jeremiah's answer is that a false prophet betrays himself by offering false security to people. "They say still unto them that despise me, the Lord hath said, Ye shall have peace." Or again: "They say unto every one that walketh after the imagination of his own heart, No evil shall come upon you." The false prophet preaches security to those who make their own inclinations the law of life and who thereby despise and defy God. The prophecy is false because a life which defies the laws of life in order to gain security destroys what it is seeking to establish. The mark of false prophecy is that it assures the sinner peace and security within terms of his sinful ambitions. True prophecy has the function of revealing the true laws of life to the sinner, and discovering to his blind eyes how he increases his insecurity by taking the law into his own hands for the purpose of establishing himself in an insecure world.

I

The most basic need of the human spirit is the need for security and the most fundamental problem of religion is the problem of meeting this need. In a true religion, faith in the ultimate meaningfulness of existence, grounded in a God who transcends the caprices and contingencies of the physical order and who is capable of overcoming the chaos created by human sin, is the final security of the human spirit. In false religion this ultimate security is prematurely appropriated and corrupted so that it assures man peace in his sins and not through the forgiveness of his sins. To understand the importance of this distinction it is necessary to analyse the whole imperilled nature of the human enterprise.

Man's insecurity lies first of all in the determinate and finite character of human existence amidst the immensities of the physical world and the caprices of nature. When he surveys the heavens, the work of God's hands, the moon and the stars which He hath ordained, he is overcome with a sense of his own insignificance: "What is man that thou shouldst be mindful of him?" The summer's heat and the winter's cold, the capricious storm or the equally unpredictable attack of unseen disease germs, may destroy his life. To the perils of the natural order must be added the perils of the social order. At any moment man may become the victim of the greed, the cruelty, and the thoughtless passions of his fellows. The fury of war may claim his life. He is, as was St. Paul, "In peril by land, in peril by sea, in peril of false brethren." Unable to live without a sense of the meaningfulness of his existence, his confidence in meaning is constantly imperilled by the chaos which threatens to engulf him. The chaos may be represented by the capricious forces of nature which seem to take no account of his significance, his hopes and his dreams. In the words of Goethe: *Die Elemente hassen das Gebild her Menschenhand.* Or the chaos may erupt out of the sinful forces of his society; for all human society seems but a tentative peace and uneasy armistice between conflicting interests and passions.

In consequence of these perils the need of security is a basic need of human life. I remember how wonderful was the experience of my boyhood when we ran to the barn, warned by ominous clouds of an approaching storm, and then heard the wind and the rain beating outside while safe and dry under the eaves of the haymow. The experience had actual religious overtones. The safety and shelter of the haymow were somehow symbolic of all security against dark and tempestuous powers. The words of the Psalmist, committed to memory in confirmation class, achieved a sudden and vivid relevance: "Thou shalt not be afraid for the terror by night; nor for the arrow that flieth by day; nor for the pestilence that walketh in darkness; nor for the destruction that wasteth at noonday. There shall no evil befall thee, neither shall any plague come nigh thy dwelling." This word of the psalm is, incidentally, a perfect illustration of all the illusions which may arise from an ultimate religious faith. When faith in an ultimate security is couched in symbolic expressions which suggest protection from all immediate perils, it is easy to be tempted to the illusion that the child of God will be accorded special protection from the capricious forces of the natural world or special immunity from the vindictive passions of angry men. Any such faith is bound to suffer disillusionment. Nor does it deserve moral respect.

Stoic indifference toward the varying vicissitudes of mortal existence is preferable to lobbying, with whining entreaties, in the courts of the Almighty, hoping for special favours which are not granted to ordinary mortals or to godless men. The ultimate security of a noble faith lies in the assurance that "all things must work together for good," but not that all things are of themselves good, or that the faithful will escape vicissitudes which are of themselves evil rather than good. Those who know and love God understand that the meaning of life lies rooted in a power too great and good to be overcome by the momentary anarchies of history or by the periodic suggestions of chaos and meaninglessness which arise from man's strange relationship to nature's blind and morally indifferent forces. St. Paul expresses this idea

97

perfectly in a glorious passage in Romans: "For I am persuaded, that neither death, nor life, nor angels, nor principalities, nor powers, nor things present, nor things to come, nor height, nor depth, nor any other creature, shall be able to separate us from the love of God, which is in Christ Jesus our Lord." Every possible peril and evil is anticipated—and discounted, because it cannot destroy the faith, that the love of God gives meaning to life.

II

The sin of man arises from his effort to establish his own security; and the sin of the false prophet lies in the effort to include this false security within the ultimate security of faith. The false security to which all men are tempted is the security of power. The primary insecurity of human life arises from its weakness and finiteness. Man is a frail little insect buffeted by forces vaster than he. Man is a defenseless creature, the prey of armed and brutal men. What is more natural than that he should seek to transmute his weakness into strength? That he should desire enough power to hold the enmity of nature at bay and to intimidate his human foes? So natural is this that we will concede its necessity and refrain from challenging it by pacifistic moralising. Surrounded by armed foes, the defenseless nation will obey a natural impulse of survival and arm itself for defense, unless it should discover, as have some animals, that the best defense is defenselessness. But, if it is wise, it will not draw self-righteous conclusions from this paradoxical strategy or imagine that all men and nations can adopt it with impunity.

Nor is man's triumph over nature evil of itself. The whole history of civilisation is a chronicle of man's increasingly effective exploitation of natural forces for his own ends. Prometheus, the firebringer, is the true hero of the human epic. Every technical advance has had the effect of strengthening the weak human body. The human eye can now see into the stars, the human voice carry to the ends of the earth; human feet have been transmuted into incredibly speedy wheels; and the wings of birds have been added to human equipment. The automatic machine has enhanced the dexterity of human hands; and power machinery has given the frail human body the strength of a thousand giants. While some of these technical advances have exchanged new perils for the old ones, no one would be so perverse as to question the beneficent effect of this total development, particularly not if the medical sciences are included through which the human body found protection against the "pestilence that wasteth at noonday" and from all the stealthy enemies of health which have assailed man's flesh.

III

Considering how natural and inevitable is the impulse to seek security through power and how successfully power achieves its desired object, it is not surprising that there should be many false prophets who encourage men to trust this security, assuring them "no evil shall befall thee" and "the Lord hath said ye shall have peace." Why is their prophecy false? Because they do not see to what degree the security of power leads to both injustice and pride.

All power leads to pride and injustice; to the pride of "them that despise me," the pride of men who have forgotten that they are creatures and that no creaturely human strength is strong enough to make nature purely the servant of man rather than his nemesis; to the injustice of those who create their security at the expense of the security and freedom of others. The sin of pride, to which the prophets of Israel were so sensitive, is more obvious in our day than in theirs. Yet there are fewer prophets to recognise and challenge it. If this age is essentially irreligious, the basic cause of our irreligion is our sense of self-sufficiency. The achievements of science and technics have beguiled us into a false complacency. We have forgotten the frailty of man. We have overlooked the fact that no medicine for senility can be found by even the most advanced science. We have failed to consider that the mystery of death still challenges human pride; that man, for all of his enhanced physical strength, continues to be as grass which flourisheth in the morning and in the evening is cut down and withereth. He still "brings his years to an end like a tale that is told." Sometimes this abyss of death suddenly opens before the proud modern and the peril of meaninglessness threatens his security. That is the significance of the philosophies of pessimism which periodically break through the optimism and self-sufficiency of modern irreligion and try, with Bertrand Russell, to erect a structure of meaning upon the "firm foundation of unyielding despair." No ultimate sense of meaning can be gained from the conquest of nature; for, in the words of a medical leader, more realistic than most moderns, "nature intends to kill man and will succeed in the end."

Pride as a consequence of power gives man a false security. Thus it enhances his insecurity. This is as true of collective man as of individual man. Modern civilisation, which beguiled itself in its youth with the dreams of eternal progress current in the seventeenth and eighteenth centuries, is facing a more premature senility than any previous culture. The forces of human rationality, which it trusted to arrest the decay to which all civilisations seem subject, have accentuated the processes of decadence. Human

reason has sharpened the anarchies of nature and sin
and made the resulting conflicts more deadly. There
is a curious irony in this denouement. It is such a vivid
portrayal of the self-defeat of human pride. Here is
mortal man, darkly conscious of the capricious and
arbitrary character of human fate. He thinks his
own reason is an eternal and universal force, set
against the contingencies of nature, only to discover
that human reason remains a servant of the passions
of nature within him and a victim of the caprices of
nature about him. Nothing in world history illustrates
more clearly than contemporary history the meaning
of the prophetic word: "Surely men of low degree
are a vanity and men of high degree are a lie. God
hath spoken once, twice have I heard this that power
belongeth unto God."

Injustice is as inevitably a consequence of power as
pride. The life which seeks to transcend its creatureliness and make itself the centre of existence offends
not only against God, who is the centre and source
of existence, but against other life which has a rightful place in the harmony of the whole. Security
through power means insecurity for those who lack
power. It is interesting how clearly the prophets saw
the relation to each other of power, pride and injustice; and how unfailingly they combined their
strictures against the religious sin of pride and the

social sin of injustice. Modern exponents of the "social gospel" are usually not as penetrating in their insights. They see only the sin of injustice but not its source. Kings and emperors, oligarchs and aristocrats, empires and civilisation all illustrate this perennial sin of all men: Seeking to transcend the insecurities of finiteness through power, they involve themselves in the insecurities of sin. Their power, by which they intend to protect themselves against other life, tempts them to destroy and oppress other life. But sooner or later the oppressed life is endowed by the spirit of justice—and vengeance—with a strength that complements its weakness. Jeremiah accurately describes this process of history and the rise and fall of empires in the simple words: "Woe unto them that spoil and are not spoiled; when they cease to spoil they will be spoiled."

How curiously nature and sin are involved in this process; for human imagination transmutes nature's harmless will-to-live into a sinful will-to-power. But the will-to-power always hides behind the natural will-to-live. France's vindictive oppression of her German foe was prompted by genuine fears, lest she be destroyed if the foe should arise and regain his strength. But the spirit of vengeance against this injustice was the very force by which the foe arose; and now that he has arisen he seems to dream of gaining sufficient strength to become forever impregnable. The Germans speak with religious fervour of an "eternal Germany"; but the policies by which they seek to gain this strength make the whole of Europe insecure. In this insecurity one may already discern the forces which will destroy German security before it is fairly established. "Eternal" Germany is haunted by the spectre of dissolution; which is the reason why she dreams so fantastically of her eternity and seeks so frantically to establish it.

This is the vicious circle in which sin inevitably involves the man or nation who tries to gain immortality. The moralist will draw the obvious conclusion from such a portrayal of the facts that the nations ought to learn what individuals have long since learned: that collective security is preferable to the anarchy of conflicting interests. Such a conclusion is legitimate and necessary. But it does not solve the total problem. Among the false prophets who say, "Ye shall have assured peace in this place." are both realists and moralists. The realists condone the struggle for power as an inevitable extension of the will-to-live and therefore morally permissible. The moralists believe that because such a struggle is obviously suicidal it should not be too difficult to dissuade men from it. The moralistic prophet is not as false as the first. He is at least capable of speaking a warning "Thus said the Lord" to particular nations at particular times. Yet this moralism is false prophecy. Its error can be most briefly described as its failure to understand what Christian theology has meant by original sin. It does not see that man is not free to extricate himself from the vicious circle of sin, even if he recognises it as a vicious circle. This is true, if for no other reason, because even though he can see how others are involved in it, he never believes himself involved. In himself the will-to-power always seems to be perfectly justified by impulses of survival and policies of defense. It is this very blindness and self-deception which constitutes the mystery of sin. For it is really a mystery. No one, not even the most astute psychologist, has ever made a perfectly convincing anaylsis of the comparative degrees of ignorance and dishonesty which enter into it.

IV

Once this is recognised, the prophet is under compulsion to speak a woe, not only upon specific forms of human injustice but upon the human heart for its perennial injustice and the recurring tragedy of its self-defeating sin. Then he will be able to offer no civilisation "assured peace in this place." Then man will be forced more and more to rely upon an ultimate mercy to resolve the paradoxes of his life. Perhaps there is an equal danger of false prophecy in such a word of judgment upon all life and every civilisation. Such a prophecy may fail to explore the moral possibilities which actually exist in every human civilisation. Individuals differ in the degrees of ego-centricity which they express. Nations differ in the wisdom with which they seek to gain a more ultimate collective security in place of the tentative security of their own power. There is always some possibility of fulfilling the law of life, which is the law of love. Individuals may, on occasion, forget themselves and discover that self-realisation is the consequence of such forgetfulness; and that it is most surely its consequence if it is not its designed and desired end. To the prophet's task, therefore, belongs the duty of revealing the way of God more perfectly. That means suggesting alternatives for specific sins.

A dominant class must be told that there is no security in increasing oppression of a resentful oppressed class. Sooner or later injustice will create the force of vengeance by which it is destroyed. The nation must be told that no nation can be strong enough to protect itself against all of its foes, particularly since its strength arouses new enemies against it. Individuals must be taught the self-defeating character of every form of ego-centricity. The prophet Jeremiah defines one of the marks of the good prophet as his ability to cause "my people to hear my words, then should they have turned them from their evil ways." Moral counsel belongs to the task of true prophecy. But if this moral counsel is not informed by a profound understanding of the human heart it will be easily tempted to regard some partial victory over human sin as the ultimate victory. It will fail to see how perennially and inevitably the human soul is involved in the self-defeat of sin, no matter what level of righteousness it achieves.

Thus the false prophet of our day imagines that commercial and trading nations have discovered the law of mutuality by which social enmity is destroyed. They glorify the prudent internationalism of the trader. Yet a trading civilisation is involved in more bitter international quarrels than any civilisation of history. Thus too the false prophets of our day speak of our bourgeois civilisation as a "Christian" civilisation because it is democratic, imagining that democracy represents something of the eternal and ultimate spirit of love. These same false prophets claim God for their civilisation and pronounce maledictions upon any one who suggests that even a democratic civilisation may stand under the judgment and the doom of God. A New York minister, whose sermon was recently reported in a metropolitan daily, spoke in this spirit. He said: "Let us not listen to the croakings of the pessimists who prophesy the end of our civilisation. God's arm is not shortened that he cannot save. Let us implore his aid in our extremity and we will live to praise his name." Thus a modern sermoniser expresses sentiments strikingly similar to the ancient words which fell under Jeremiah's strictures: "They say unto them that despise me, the Lord hath said ye shall have peace— no evil shall befall you."

The false prophet does not see that democracy may be little more than the luxury of a stable civilisation, in which the social struggle has been mitigated for the time being because one side has so much power that the other side cannot challenge it, or because there has been so much comparative affluence that injustice is obscured by the comparative comfort of the oppressed. But when a contracting economy destroys the total wealth of a society and when the stabilised social equilibrium is disturbed, the social struggle breaks out afresh; and there is no guarantee that such a struggle may not break the forms of democratic arbitration of rights and interests.

No society and no individual can ever escape the vicious circle of the sin which aggravates human insecurity by seeking to overcome it. All societies and individuals therefore remain under the judgment and the doom of God. Their hope must therefore always lie in a mercy which is able to overrule the angry passions of men, in a Kingdom of God which will bring the kingdom of sin to naught. The more they understand this, the more will they be able to build civilisations in which the sinful aggravation of the struggle for existence is mitigated.

V

The temptations to false prophecy are so ubiquitous that any sensitive teacher of the word may well be driven to the edge of despair. It is so easy to condemn flagrant pride and to condone a subtle form of it; to outlaw overt injustice and to sanction a covert form of it; to condone the security of power because its tentative necessity is recognised; or accept injustice complacently as the price and inevitable consequence of power; or to encourage men to the illusory hope that they may build a world in which there is no power, pride or injustice. How can all of these temptations be avoided? They cannot. All of us will always have something of the false prophet in us, wherefore we ought to speak humbly. We will mistake our own dreams for the word of God. Sometimes sloth will tempt us to make a superficial analysis of the moral and social facts with which we are dealing; sometimes pride will tempt us to speak as if we had already attained or were already made perfect; sometimes cowardice will tempt us to make concessions to the immense, blind and stubborn self-righteousness with which every culture, every nation and every individual wards off the word of God.

It is instructive that the same Jeremiah who spoke so uncompromisingly against the false prophets tried to return his prophetic commission to God. He was not certain that he was worthy of it, and he doubted his courage to maintain the integrity of the word of God against the resistance of a whole generation which demanded security from religion and rejected the prophet who could offer no security on this side of repentance. His commission was returned to him by the Lord with the demand that he "separate the precious from the vile" in himself, so that he might be worthy to be a prophet. Thus the Church can disturb the security of sinners only if it is not itself too secure in its belief that it has the word of God. The prophet himself stands under the judgment which he preaches. If he does not know that, he is a false prophet.

Six:
THE ULTIMATE
TRUST

Thus saith the Lord; Cursed be the man that trusteth in man and maketh flesh his arm, and whose heart departeth from the Lord. For he shall be like the heath in the desert, and shall not see when good cometh; but shall inhabit the parched places in the wilderness, in a salt land and not inhabited. Blessed is the man that trusteth in the Lord, and whose hope the Lord is. For he shall be as a tree planted by the waters, and that spreadeth out her roots by the river, and shall not see when the heat cometh, but her leaf shall be green; and shall not be careful in the year of drought, neither shall cease from yielding fruit. The heart is deceitful above all things and desperately wicked: who can know it?

Jeremiah 17:5–9.

6:   THE ULTIMATE
                        TRUST

I T IS significant that the profoundest
expressions of prophetic religion come out of periods
of catastrophe. The great prophets spoke when Israel
lost its national existence. Christianity was born in
the decay of Græco-Roman culture. Augustine interpreted Christianity and gave its theology a new
foundation during the death throes of the Roman
Empire. The Protestant Reformation was roughly
synchronous with the decay of feudalism. Perhaps
some such rebirth of Christian faith will come out of
the catastrophic era in which we are living.

   The Christian religion, in its profoundest terms,
is a faith in the meaningfulness of existence which is
able to defy the chaos of any moment, because the
basis of its trust is not in any of the constructs of
human genius or any of the achievements of human
diligence which arise periodically to imposing heights
and tempt men to put their trust in their own virtues
and abilities. Christianity believes in a God who
created the world and will redeem it; but it knows
that the purposes of God may be momentarily and

periodically frustrated by human wickedness. It knows the heart of man to "be deceitful above all things and desperately wicked." The basis of its trust and hope is, therefore, not in some natural increase of human virtue or some final achievement of human intelligence. Christianity, at its best, is, therefore, not involved in chaos and confusion when the imposing structures of human contrivance fall, as they inevitably do and must. The chaos of the destruction does not tempt it to a sense of ultimate confusion. It knows that "the world passeth away and the lusts thereof," and that the self-destruction in which the world's empires become periodically involved is but a proof of the immutability of God's laws and the power of his sovereignty, which men defy at their peril.

Yet so great is the power of human pride that again and again, even within terms of the Christian faith, man places his essential trust not in the ultimate character of God but in some achievement of the human spirit. The temptation to do this is particularly great when these achievements are especially imposing; when the edifices of human genius have achieved a stability which seems to suggest their indestructibility. Hence periods of prosperity inevitably lead to the corruption of the Christian faith, while periods of adversity prompt men to probe more deeply into the nature and meaning of human life, to move from the parched places and plant their tree of faith by the water, where the roots may reach the river and where the leaf may remain green despite the year of drought. Thus periods of adversity are the seasons of a genuine renewal of the Christian religion.

I

Faith is always imperilled on the one side by despair and on the other side by optimism. Of these two enemies of faith, optimism is the more dangerous. Few people live in permanent despair. They will construct some little cosmos in the seeming chaos of existence to give meaning to their life. The greater danger is lest the cosmos, from which they derive their sense of meaning, be too tentative and tenuous to support the idea of meaning in the great crises of existence. Optimism is essentially the construction of such a little cosmos. Optimism and human self-sufficiency are almost identical. Most optimistic creeds, when reduced to their essentials, prove themselves to be confidence in some human virtue or capacity. The optimistic man trusts life because he believes in his nation, or in his culture, or in the goodness of his church, or in the goodness of pious men, or in the capacity of human reason for infinite growth, or in the ability of one particular class to build a civilisation which will be free of the evils by which all previous civilisations have destroyed themselves. Each new creed of human optimism is but a variation of the basic creed of all those who "trust in man and make flesh their arm." So great is the power of human pride and so inevitable the blindness of this pride that the illusions of this optimism do not become apparent until history itself destroys the very force or source of meaning which men have trusted. The victory of the Christian faith over humanistic optimism is consequently dependent upon an adequate understanding of the crises and catastrophes of history in which men have seen more clearly than they were able to see when the sunshine of their own genius blinded their eyes.

II

Primitive man derived his sense of a meaningful existence from his relation to his tribe and nation. Nothing existed beyond it, except the god who had chosen it and who would redeem it. The early Hebraic conception of Yahweh's peculiar relation to his chosen people is but a perfect elaboration of primitive faith everywhere. The nation could not perish because God was with it and in it. The fact that the nation cannot be god to primitive man, without the suggestion that a god who transcended the nation claimed it as its very own, is an instructive indication of the complexity of the problem of the meaning of life. Even in early culture there was some realisation of the hazardous and insecure character of all human existence, of even the seemingly eternal collective existence. Therefore a god greater than the nation must guarantee its permanence and worth. The first prophet who laid bare the logic of this insecurity in the religious security of Israel was Amos. Emphasising the transcendence of God over Israel, he insisted that the same god who had called Israel to a peculiar relationship might destroy it, if it transgressed his laws. The day of Yahweh would be "darkness and not light." If Yahweh was greater than Israel his hand might be seen in the destinies of other peoples besides his own: "Are ye not as the children of the Ethiopians unto me, O children of Israel? saith the Lord. Have not I brought up Israel out of the land of Egypt? and the Philistines from Caphtor and the Syrians from Kir?"

The interpretation of God and His relation to human history in the thought of Amos preceded the catastrophe which helped to inspire the prophecies of Jeremiah and the Second Isaiah. Perhaps the fact that Amos anticipated the catastrophe is proof of the ability of profound religious faith to see the insecurity of human achievements even before history fully reveals it. In fact the religious insights of Jeremiah and the Second Isaiah, through which the catastrophe that befell Israel became the occasion for the deepening of religious faith, would hardly have been possible without the preparations for it in the pre-exilic prophetic movement, beginning with Amos. The anticipations of Amos are a convincing refutation of the critics of religion who think it is merely a compensation for failure and defeat. The Hebraic prophetic movement found a source of the meaning of human existence which not only transcended any possible chaos in history but actually predicted catastrophe as the inevitable consequence of man's sin against life and God. The Hebrews were the first people of ancient times to achieve national integrity in something like the modern meaning of that term; perhaps that is one reason why their religion was first to transcend nationalism. This historical achievement lends a peculiar irony to the accusations of their modern German foes, who are seeking to reconstruct a purely national religion in modern times.

The faith of this first great epoch of prophetic religion could be expressed in a paraphrase of Jeremiah's words: Cursed be the man who trusteth in collective man and imagines that the immortality of his nation compensates for the insecurity of his own life. Nations are also mortal. When the processes of nature and history, and the judgments of God overtake them, life will be meaningless, if it has not discovered a source of meaning untouched by the destruction.

III

The faith of early Christianity was apocalyptic. It waited for the second coming of Christ. It was in other words a culmination of the whole prophetic movement which regarded human history as meaningful but not as self-fulfilling or self-sufficing. The victory of good over evil was not guaranteed by anything in human nature or human history. The expression of this faith in apocalyptic symbols (the second coming of Christ) unfortunately led to chronological and historical illusions. When the hope in the second coming of the Lord was disappointed, Christianity came to terms with the world in a series of more or less unplanned compromises which culminated in its becoming a kind of new cement of social cohesion for a Roman Empire, the edifice of which was falling apart for lack of cement. Christian faith consequently became mixed with faith in Roman civilisation and justified itself partly in terms of the contributions it had made to the stability of the Empire. To the degree it did this its faith rested not upon God but upon man, in this case Roman man. The destruction of Rome shattered this complacency. In that moment St. Augustine performed a service to Christian theology, comparable to the reinterpretation of Hebrew thought in the great prophets. The Christian faith, he argued, was in no wise disturbed by the fall of Rome. On the contrary, it understood why every "earthly city" was bound to destroy itself since its principle of "self-love in contempt of God" prompted it to rebellion against God. In such a city "the glory of the incorruptible God" is changed into "the likeness of the image of a corruptible man." In other words the very weakness of the earthly city is man's self-worship, a devotion which involves the city in "wars, altercations and appetites of bloody and deadly victories." The victories are as deadly as its defeats, for "if it conquers it extols itself and so becomes its own destruction." Augustine saw the tragic aspect of human history very clearly. With the prophets he regarded human pride as the root of human injustice; and both pride and injustice as violations of the will of God. In such an interpretation of history the Christian faith was not involved in the destruction of empires but was its very principle of interpretation. Through it and by it Augustine recognised that the chaos of a period was not a meaningless chaos but a revelation of the counsels of God working themselves out in history.

Unfortunately, on the positive side of St. Augustine's doctrine he allowed a new trust in man to be conceived. He set the "city of God" against the city of the world. The principle of the city of God was "love of God in contempt of one's self." Augustine was restating, in other words, the biblical conception

of the Kingdom of God, the transcendent principle
of all moral action. Unfortunately Augustine identified this heavenly city with the church. This enabled
him to maintain the idea of the meaningfulness of
mundane history. But it also involved him in the
error of placing too great a trust in man, in this case
the redeemed man in the church. Even a man who
lives by grace remains finite and sinful, and the
church which he builds is a very human institution.
It is subject to the aberrations of particular generations and the faulty insights and sinful ambitions of
special groups and classes. The "heavenly city" of the
church happens to exist on earth and to draw its
sustenance from very earthly sources, particularly
since it easily becomes dependent upon those classes
of society who can most easily support it, that is,
those who benefit most from the injustices of any
society. Augustine, in short, was responsible for the
great heresy of Roman Catholicism, the heresy of
identifying the church with the Kingdom of God and
of making unqualified claims of divinity for this
human, historical and relative institution.

Medieval civilisation was the fruit of both the
virtue and the vice of Augustine's thought. Its trust
in God was essentially a trust in the church and in
the imposing and impressive civilisation which the
church had built. This civilisation, at its best, was
really a glorious achievement. But it was not as

Christian as it imagined itself to be. A Roman Pope may, at best, be better than a Roman Cæsar. In the greatest of medieval Popes, such as Gregory VII and Innocent III, the spirit of Christ may have been more potent than the genius of Cæsar. But since the Popes were temporal rulers the genius of Cæsar was not completely destroyed. When they claimed therefore to be, without qualification, vicars of Christ upon earth, they balanced their higher moral achievements with higher moral and religious pretensions than Cæsar. But we need not point to the Popes alone as expressions of the moral and religious peril in which the church always lives. Wherever religion is mixed with power and wherever the religious man achieves power, whether inside or outside the church, he is in danger of claiming divine sanction for the very human and frequently sinful actions, which he takes and must take. Cursed be the man that trusteth in man's church.

God gave the church its gospel and the Holy Spirit keeps faith alive in it. But human genius creates and human sin corrupts all the historical and relative forms of the church. Whenever the latter are treated as if they were the necessary forms or as if there were no distinction between them and the gospel, the church itself falls under the curse which the prophet pronounced. It falls doubly under it because its claims are doubly pretentious.

All through the medieval period Christians were not conscious of the dubious manner in which they had mixed faith in God and trust in man. Religious faith was compounded with faith in a "Christian" civilisation. The destruction of that civilisation was a new occasion for discovering the error that had been made and re-interpreting the Christian religion in the light of its New Testament meaning. Thus Protestantism was born. Ideally, Protestantism is the form of Christianity which sees the peril of human self-confidence most clearly. Protestantism does not believe in saints. It does not believe that any man can claim to have achieved the Kingdom of God by virtue of his virtues. It trusts the grace of God but not human goodness. It does not believe that the visible church can ever be identified with the Kingdom of God, though it must be admitted that practically this is frequently done. But the Protestant must violate rather than conform to the doctrine of his church to do it. Yet Protestantism is not free of the temptation to place its trust in man. It trusts the pious man. The pious man knows God's will. The pious man does God's will. The pious man sometimes suggests that if only the pagans and the heathen were as good as he, the Kingdom of God would come. The Protestant is an individualist, so he is less liable to place his trust in a culture or a civilisation, which ostensibly God has built through his servants. He does not trust the priest as the mediator between God and man. He is himself priest and prophet. That is a very dangerous pretension. What have been the historical consequences? Sometimes Protestant piety has degenerated into barren orthodoxy; sometimes into Puritan self-righteousness, of the kind described in Hawthorne's *Scarlet Letter,* for instance. Sometimes the very relative moral code of lower middle-class life has been dignified as the sign and the proof of a "God-fearing" man in Calvinistic Protestantism. Sometimes the ethics of money-getting is sanctified in the same manner. On occasion the pious Protestant is as certain that his civilisation (capitalism) is God's peculiar civilisation as the Catholic was certain of feudalism. All these aberrations give us reason to affirm anew with the prophet, "Cursed be the man that trusteth in man," even if he be pious man or, perhaps, particularly if he be pious man.

IV

The whole of modern civilisation came to the interesting conclusion that what made human beings dangerous, unjust and unreliable was precisely their religious faith. Religion had made so many false claims and had so frequently defended the indefensible in the name of faith that modern culture, with the rise of science and rationalism, conceived a new version of the old human pride. The man you can trust, it said in effect, is the intelligent man, the educated man. Let us solve the problems of mankind by universal education. Education will eliminate religious prejudice and superstition and all the injustices which flow from it. Thus the prophets of the eighteenth century dreamed of an imminent Utopia in which reason would adjust all human conflicts and reasonableness arbitrate all contests of interest.

It was a plausible dream. So plausible, that millions of moderns, particularly in America, are still convinced by it, in spite of the fact that the civilisation for which the rational idealists laid the foundation in the eighteenth century is careening at the present moment to almost certain destruction. The reason, which they hoped would triumph over all irrational impulse, turns out to be the servant of prejudice as much as its master, in even the best of men. The ubiquity of the written word, which, in the opinion of Condorcet, would bring salvation to the world, can spread vulgarity and prejudice as quickly or more quickly than it can spread enlightenment. Science can sharpen the fangs of ferocity as much as it can alleviate human pain. All of the achievements of modern science and of a higher degree of rationality are necessary and inevitable. Ignorance and obscurantism are not to be preferred to them. But "cursed be the man that trusteth in man," even if it be intelligent man or, perhaps, particularly if he be intelligent man.

For intelligence merely raises all the potencies of life, both good and evil. The first "rational" civilisation in the history of the world has run its span from birth to death more quickly than any other. Its tempo is quicker, its passions more effectively directed to achieve their end, its cruelties more highly organised and its lies more shrewdly propagated by the latest methods of propaganda.

Liberal Protestantism has a version of the old humanistic trust which represents a nice combination of the Protestant and the rationalist variation. The man to be trusted is the man who is both pious and intelligent. Piety will discipline his will to be good, and intelligence will direct the good-will to proper and socially useful ends. Such in effect is the faith of liberal Protestantism. Let it be admitted that intelligence may save the pious man from obscurantism. And that piety may save the intelligent man from futile sophistication. Yet it is barely possible, a possibility which liberal Protestantism has not considered, that piety may rob the intelligent man of his critical vigour and intelligence may destroy the indispensable naïveté of all robust religion. The fruit of this marriage may therefore be an enervated sentimentality. This is not to decry either piety or intelligence or to deny the value of the compound which contains both. Yet it is necessary to insist that this form of human goodness, as every other form, is subject to its own peculiar corruptions and to some corruptions which are not peculiar but merely the natural and inevitable corruptions of all human goodness. If you trust the intelligent pious man he may confound you by insisting that the final form of human society is a mild capitalism, joined with a mild democracy, garnished with a mild philanthropy and perfected with a genteel religion. If any hungry man should be impatient with this paradise and become a revolutionist he will be threatening not only "law and order" but the very counsels of God.

A very special form of human self-confidence developed after the war in the so-called youth-movements. Trust the young man, they declared. Old people are shrewd, designing and cowardly, and so habituated to ancient vices that the possibility of a new creation is not in them. Trust youth. It is heroic and self-sacrificing. It brings a fresh conscience to the world, and is outraged by the evils which its elders have so long accepted. There is some truth in this estimate, as there is in every preceding estimate of human capacity. The progress of the world does depend upon the vigour and hope with which each new generation approaches age-old problems. But it is significant that all these youth movements of Europe have in this latter day been captured by the various nationalistic hysterias of the Continent. It is instructive that the most fanatic disciples of fanatic religions are young people; and that the peace of Europe is imperilled most by the young people who did not know the horrors of the last war but long for the romance of the next. What could be more pitiful than this corruption of European youth? Parents and instructors are powerless against it. Human pride has taken just another form. The form is peculiar but the pride is the old sin of Adam. This pride prevents young people from realising that their "singleness" of heart is frequently the direct consequence of their emptiness of head. Cursed be the man that trusteth in the young man as the hope of the future.

The most recent form of the humanistic optimism, which has become the religion of millions, after other forms of humanism have become discredited, might be expressed in the phrase: Trust the poor man. Since he has no interests to defend he can be trusted to see the truth. Marxism is a form of humanism which has detected the illusions and dishonesties of all human cultures. It has rightly seen to what degree all cultural enterprises are related to the peculiar circumstances and the special interests of the classes which dominate a culture. It does not trust the piety of the pious man or the wisdom of the wise man. It points out, that inasfar as the pious and the wise men are also the privileged men of society, they think in terms of their privileges and not in terms of an absolute wisdom or absolute integrity. There is genuine merit in this approach to historic situations. The Marxian trust in the proletariat, as the redeemer of mankind, is not unrelated to the biblical blessing upon the poor. The biblical emphasis is primarily upon the humility of the poor, as against the arrogance of the rich and mighty. But humility of spirit is a prerequisite of integrity. Within the terms of the general and universal weakness of the human mind and the dishonesty of the human heart it may be taken for granted that the poor man sees the ultimate issues of life more truly than the powerful or rich man. Therefore Jesus counsels us not to lay up treasures on earth and not to serve both God and Mammon. One might add to this gospel blessing upon the poor, an appreciation of the poor of the earth as having a superior dynamic to the satiated. The hungry man may be driven by hunger to seek a world in which none are hungry. Thus by a curious alchemy of the spirit dreams of the Kingdom of God may be distilled out of pangs of hunger so that they are something more than merely physical desire.

There is therefore a very good reason to appreciate the Marxian trust in the proletariat as a class which stands under a special destiny, as being fated to see and to do things in the crisis of society which the wise cannot see and will not do. But this trust in the poor man can be only a provisional and not an ultimate trust. A final confidence in the victory of good over evil cannot be based upon it. The reason for this mistrust can be simply stated. If the poor man is generally trusted as a social force of high destiny in society he will achieve the power to overturn society and build a new social order. He will then cease to be the poor man and will become the powerful man. The prophets who lead him in the wilderness will become the priest-kings of the new order. The new social order may be immeasurably better than the old one but it will not be free of the temptation to corrupt and to misuse power. Perhaps in this paradise of the poor man's dreams, the one prophet who has gained all the power will kill his fellow prophets. Stalin will condemn Kamenev and Zinoviev to death and Trotzky to exile. Only a person who allows unconscious utopian illusions to be transmuted into conscious lies will be able to view such contemporary facts without admitting that a too unqualified trust in the poor man as the redeemer will be the very force by which the poor man becomes untrustworthy. "Cursed be the man that trusteth in man"—even the poor man, particularly if the poor man has become the powerful man, which he will become if he is fully trusted.

Trust no man. Every man has his own capacities but also his own weaknesses. Every historic group in society has its own unique contribution to make. But there is no form of human goodness which cannot be and will not be corrupted, particularly in the day of its success. Let the wise man destroy the superstitions of the priest, and the poor man disprove the pride of the wise man; but then a new prophet must arise to convict the priest-king of the poor of the perennial sins of mankind to which he is also subject.

Ultimate confidence in the goodness of life can, in other words, not rest upon confidence in the goodness of man. If that is where it rests it is an optimism which will suffer ultimate disillusionment. Romanticism will be transmuted into cynicism, as it has always been in the world's history. The faith of a Christian is something quite different from this optimism. It is trust in God, in a good God who created a good world, though the world is not now good; in a good God, powerful and good enough finally to destroy the evil that men do and redeem them of their sins. This kind of faith is not optimism. It does not, in fact, arise until optimism breaks down and men cease to trust in themselves that they are righteous. Faced with the indubitable fact of human history that there is no human vitality which is not subject to decay and no human virtue which is not subject to corruption, hope in the meaningfulness of human existence must be nourished by roots which go deeper than the deserts of history, with their periodic droughts.

The Christian faith in the goodness of God is not to be equated with confidence in the virtue of man. But neither is it a supernaturalism and otherworldliness which places its hope in another world because it finds this world evil. Every distinction between an essentially good eternity and an essentially evil finiteness is foreign to the Christian faith. When Christians express their faith in such terms they have been corrupted by other types of religion. For the Christian who really understands his faith, life is worth living and this world is not merely a "vale of tears." He is able to discern the goodness of creation beneath the corruptions of human sin. Nor will he be driven to despair by the latter; for the God in whom he believes is the redeemer as well as creator. He has confidence, in other words, that evil cannot overwhelm the good. His happiness will be partly derived from the knowledge that the evil which other men do him is not very different from the evil which he does to others. He will not suffer the tortures of the cynics who falsely equate their ideals with their achievements and regard their fellowmen with bitterness because the latter fail to measure up to their ideals, but are unconscious of the degree to which they themselves fall short of them. The best antidote for the bitterness of a disillusioned trust in man is disillusionment in the self. This is the disillusionment of true repentance.

132

Seven:
CHILDHOOD AND MATURITY

And Jesus called a little child unto him and set him in the midst of them, and said, Verily I say unto you, Except ye be converted, and become as little children, ye shall not enter into the kingdom of heaven.   *Matthew 18:2–3.*

When I was a child, I spake as a child, I understood as a child, I thought as a child: but when I became a man I put away childish things.   *I Corinthians 13:11.*

Brethren, be not children in understanding: howbeit in malice be ye children, but in understanding be men.
   I Corinthians 14:20.

7: CHILDHOOD AND
MATURITY

I

JESUS seems to place a premium upon childlikeness. St. Paul implies the necessity of maturity. The superficial contradiction of these two emphases, which St. Paul resolves in his admonition, "Be not children in understanding, howbeit in malice be ye children, but in understanding be men," points to a profound and perennial problem of human life. Maturity is both good and evil. It is both life and death.

Maturity is life. The mature man understands his world and himself better than the child. His reason grasps the relation of things to each other in their causal sequences. His judgment is capable of significant choices. His memory, social and individual, appropriates the experience and achievements of the past. His imagination anticipates the future. The child-man, unable to understand the relation of things to each other, ascribes an ultimate source to every natural event, thus peopling his world with spirits, monsters, gods, devils and other mysterious potencies. Maturer understanding discerns the regularities of natural processes and learns to interpret the world in terms of dependable causation rather than mysterious caprice. Childhood cannot see beyond its time and place. Maturity extends the range of its knowledge to larger areas of life and experience. Maturity is thus the fulfilment of the promise of creation. It represents a larger life than childhood.

Maturity is death. The human body begins slowly to die, shortly after it has reached its full growth at twenty-five years or thereabouts. Most athletic games, with the possible exception of golf, are the province of youth. Fortunately the mind continues to develop in a decaying body. But even the spiritual capacities of man may decay with age. Maturity may mean atrophy of the imagination, loss of the unity and serenity of childhood, degeneration from sincerity to deviousness, from expectancy and eagerness to cynicism and disillusionment.

Since maturity may mean death as well as life, it is obvious that something of the genius of childhood must be retained and recaptured as we grow into maturity. That is the significance of all the myths of religion which picture the ideal of end of life, like unto the beginning; the ultimate consummation of the Kingdom of God like the paradisiacal genesis. Perhaps the difference between childishness and childlikeness is that the latter recaptures rather than retains the simplicities and profundities of childhood. We cannot merely retain the early simplicity. We cannot be, but we must be "converted and become," as little children. The greater complexity, the wider intellectual range, the more detailed knowledge of maturity means death if something of the simplicity, unity and profundity of childhood is not constantly recaptured. In that sense a profound religion makes demands which defy the counsels of sophisticated modernity, intent upon intellectual maturity alone and blind to the price which it has paid for its sophistication.

II

The unity of a child's life is akin to animal serenity. The harmonies of nature have not been disturbed in it, though it must be admitted that the youngest human infant reveals elements of freedom which make bovine serenity impossible. The child is not at war with itself. With the growth of reason and the consequent growth of freedom the alternatives which present themselves to human choice grow in bewildering complexity. Any unity which is achieved must be a unity which holds a great profusion of impulses and desires under the check of a central will.

The problem of maturity is not only to achieve unity amidst complexity of impulses but to overcome the particular conflict between the IS and the OUGHT of life, between the ideal possibilities to which freedom encourages man and the drive of egoism, which reason sharpens rather than assuages. Thus every adult life experiences the reality of what is expressed in the myth of the Fall. The rational freedom with which man is endowed represents an ideal possibility of harmonising the forces of nature upon a higher level than they achieve in nature. But this ideal possibility is not realised. Reason distintegrates nature's harmonies without being able to reconstruct a pure harmony upon a higher level. Therefore man is estranged from himself and discovers that there is a law in his members which wars against the law that is in his mind.

Since this conflict in man is never completely resolved maturity means the loss not only of childlike innocency and unity but of childlike sincerity. A child does not pretend to be other than it is. It centres its life in itself and does not claim to do otherwise. Gradually the larger world is disclosed to the maturing mind. This world suggests a community of values greater than the self, which it ought to serve; but it also reveals a multitude of forces and an abundance of life which can be brought into the service of the self. Thus the simple egocentricity of the child grows into egotism. The self that had been only the centre of the self tries to make itself the centre of its world. The self is obviously too petty to undertake such an enterprise with complete self-assurance. It knows its existence to be justified only as it finds its subordinate place in a total scheme of life greater than itself. But this knowledge is unable to overcome the drive of egotism. Hence the self is tempted to hide its desire to dominate the world behind its pretended devotion to the world. All mature moral conduct is therefore infected with an element of dishonesty and insincerity. The lie is always intimately related to the sin of egotism. Adult character is forced by its own inner contradictions to pretend to be something which it is not. The devil is a liar. This insincerity in adult life is a part of the Fall. It is not an inherited infection but it is nevertheless a recurring one. No degree of conscious moral striving can completely eliminate it.

The difference between childlike sincerity and adult dishonesty is portrayed with particular vividness in the collective history of man. Primitive tribes live for themselves and fight for their existence against external foes. They do not justify these conflicts to themselves or to their foes. They are self-justifying. Advanced civilisations look out upon a larger world than their own life. Invariably they have both an imperialistic and a moral attitude toward this world. They seek to dominate life beyond the boundaries of their own state; but they also feel themselves the bearers and inheritors of values which transcend their national existence. When their national existence is threatened, or when an imperial impulse prompts them to extend their dominions, they always insist that it is not their national existence or the extension of their dominion which is at stake but *Kultur,* or democracy, or white civilisation, or Nordic culture. These pretensions are never wholly untrue, since maturity knows nothing of a purely discreet existence in men or nations. Every individual life is organically related to and the servant of organisations of life beyond itself. Yet these pretensions are never as simply true as the idealists pretend. Nations do not fight if they do not feel their national existence or their national pride jeopardised, though they may rise to the knowledge that the best protection of the self is devotion to a system of security, the advantages of which transcend this immediate purpose. But where the larger value is not immediately and obviously to the advantage of the more immediate one, devotion to it is qualified. This constitutional short-sightedness and dishonesty of nations has made the achievement of an international government impossible to the present time. Superficial cynics sometimes regard the hypocrisies of nations as merely the dishonest devices of statesmen. It is true of course that the interests of ruling classes accentuate this native dishonesty; but it is basically a natural and inevitable quality of mature existence. Tribes may be honest; but empires are dishonest. This fact alone makes nonsense of all simple moralistic ideas of progress. The warfare of modern man is so terrible not only because his intelligence has perfected the instruments of conflict and made them more deadly, but also because maturity has forced him into a curious hypocritical fanaticism. He can be so ruthless to his foe because he regards the foe as a peril not merely to his existence but to all high and holy values of life.

If the complexity and dishonesty of adult life are a constitutional defect it may seem futile to demand of man that he "be converted and become as a child." Indeed, no mature religion will expect what modern liberal religion has expected of man: that the recognition of his sins will lead to their complete elimination. A mature religion will know that it is dealing with something more stubborn and mysterious in human wrongdoing than some easily corrected sloth or malice. It will recognise the reality of "original sin" in other words. If it does recognise this it will have something more than a simple moral command as its plan of salvation. Yet the command to be converted and become as little children is an imperative. Dishonesty is not normative because it is general; nor is egotism right though it is the law of existence. No man can return to the innocency and unity of childhood; yet he cannot escape judgment upon his life, his egotism and his hypocrisy from a perspective, of which the innocency of childhood is a symbol. The man who sees in childhood the promise of what life ought to be, and the outline of what life truly is, has discerned one of the profoundest truths of the Christian religion. God is both the creator and the fulfilment of life. Life must move forward to what it was at the beginning. But it must move forward. Infantilism is psychopathic. There is no possibility of remaining as little children. There is only a possibility of "becoming" as little children.

To become as a little child cannot mean to recapture its innocency. To repent and be converted cannot mean to achieve perfect honesty. It must mean to achieve the honesty of knowing that we are not honest. To repent and be converted cannot mean that we will be emancipated from all selfishness. No spiritual insight or discipline can wholly free man of the inclination of human reason to extend the range of the self-regarding impulses with which nature has endowed him. But the repentant man, who knows both his dishonesty and his selfishness, will be able to check these tendencies and thus prevent life from developing a consistent hypocrisy and egotism. The unity toward which we strive cannot be the perfect unity from which we have come, because it is a unity within complexity. There is thus in the Christian religion a challenge to a higher honesty and morality and the consciousness of an unattained purity which man cannot achieve himself but which lies in the hands of God to impart. In the Parable

142

of the Vineyard those who have achieved much are as greatly in need of God's grace as those who have achieved little. The validity of this idea cannot be doubted in the light of the plight of human spirituality, though it is an offence to simple moralists. Dishonest, selfish, proud and disquieted maturity must regard the innocency of childhood as the norm of life, even though it is an unattainable norm; and as the outline of life's final fulfilment, though resources greater than any man's are required for its fulfilment. "With man this is impossible, with God all things are possible."

III

We are standing at a crisis in our social history in which political and social forces are strangely divided into two camps, in both of which the relation of childhood and maturity is not fully understood. The fascists seek to escape the complexities of modern civilisation by returning to childhood; the communists are more correct in wishing to go forward to a higher justice but wrong in imagining that perfect innocency is a possibility for man's natural history.

Modern fascism seeks to overcome the complexities, disunities and disintegrations of modern society by a return to tribal simplicity. Ludwig Klages, a typical philosopher of modern Germany, significantly regards the mind as a disease which disintegrates the simple animal harmonies of nature, as indeed it does. But when a modern nation uses all the technical arts of propaganda and organisation to force life back into its primitive unity and seeks to turn the rational process suicidally upon itself, it generates psychopathic aberrations. Romantic primitivism is a false escape from the perils of maturity. A man cannot be a child. A modern nation cannot force itself into the mould of a primitive tribe. The consequence of such an effort is not child-like innocency but the sadism of a concentration camp.

There is something equally abortive in the effort of a fascistic *Realpolitik* to escape the dishonesties and pretensions of political life and frankly and brutally to avow its egoistic ambitions. If liberal politics represents a maturity which has not discovered its own sins, then fascistic politics is a form of infantilism which seeks to escape dishonesty by disavowing all the higher loyalties to which men and nations have been only partially true. That also is a false way of salvation. A modern nation cannot escape its obligations to a civilisation greater than itself, even though it be recognised that it is never as loyal to these obligations as it ought to be and claims to be. An honesty which destroys the norms by which dishonesty is discovered may achieve an internal unity but at the expense of external anarchy.

144

Modern fascistic nationalism significantly accentuates the anarchy between nations as it seeks to overcome the anarchy within nations.

In comparison with these primitivistic tendencies in reactionary politics communism and radicalism represent health. Marxism seeks to overcome the disintegration of modern society by pressing forward to a new and higher form of integration. That is the proper strategy of maturity. Nor is the hope vain that modern society may be able to find a new form of unity, more compatible with the necessities of a technical civilisation. Communist theory is wrong only in that part of its thought in which all modernism is wrong. It is utopian. It imagines that perfect innocency, a new childhood, lies at the end of the social process. It thinks itself capable of creating a society in which all tensions are resolved and the final root of human anarchy is eliminated. If that were really possible its new society would not be the beginning of history, as it fondly imagines, but its end. For the dynamic energies of human life, which destroy the harmonies of nature, are also the creative forces of history. That is a paradox which has not dawned upon the consciousness of any simple-minded modern, whether liberal or radical. The fabric of history is woven upon a loom which has greater dimensions than any known history. No simple victory of good over evil in history is possible. Every new energy of life and every higher creative force can be, and will be, a force of distintegration as well as of integration. The realisation of this fact distinguishes the apocalyptic hopes of prophetic religion from the utopias of modernity. The problem of good and evil cannot be completely resolved in history.

IV

We have considered the serenity, unity and sincerity of the child as normative for life. That has suggested the whole range of moral and social problems which mankind faces. But we have not considered, except by implication, the cultural problems of history. For these we must regard the profundity of the child as normative. The most charming characteristic of childhood is the penchant of the child for simple but profound questions. Every child is a born theologian, which may be one reason why moderns regard theologians as obscurantists. The child is a theologian rather than a scientist. It is confused and uncertain about secondary and natural causes; but it is interested in primary and ultimate ones. It is less interested in tracing the causal sequences of the evolutionary chain than in inquiring when and why the world began.

In a recent book entitled *Conversations with Children* a breakfast dialogue between father and six-year-old daughter was reported which I am forced to quote from memory. It ran something like this:

"Father, why was I born?"
"I don't know, my child; only God knows."
"Did God want me to be born?"
"I think so."
"Was God born?"
"No, God was not born."
"If God was not born, why did he want me to be born?"
"Now be quiet, you little busybody."
"Why don't you answer my questions, you old lazybody?"

These simple questions of a little girl are perfect examples of childlike profundity. They all concern themselves with the problem of ultimate meaning: "Why was I born?" and with the relation of the infinite to the finite: "If God was not born, why did he want me to be born?" The questions of the meaning of life and of the relation of the finite to the infinite fairly exhaust the whole range of religious thought and life. The second question is suggested by the first, because every conception of meaning points to sources and fulfilments of meaning which transcend the finite world.

Religious literalism seeks to preserve childlike profundity in religion by giving simple and childlike answers to childlike questions. It thinks that the mythical answers to childlike questions are adequate scientific answers. It tries to insist that, because the idea of creation is true, it is also true that God created the world in six days; and that because the story of the Fall is true, therefore the account of the serpent and the apple in the garden is actual history. Thus it corrupts ultimate religious insights into a bad science. It tries to make mythical explanations of the ultimate "why" into scientific explanations of the immediate "how." This is a form of cultural primitivism as baneful as the social primitivism of reactionary politics.

The culture of modernity is a reaction to this kind of primitivism. It is unfortunately a new childishness which imagines that superficial answers to profound questions are sufficient. The child asks questions without claiming to know the answers. The adolescent thinks he knows the answers. The adolescent sophistication of modernity expresses itself in finding scientific answers for religious questions; in thinking that analyses of historical sequences and natural causation are an adequate approach to the problem of the meaning of life. It believes that the world is self-derived and self-explanatory because it is always possible to find a previous cause for every subsequent event.

The childlikeness of an adequate religion lies not on this but on the other side of sophistication. It is not the childlikeness of primitive ignorance but the childlikeness of a wisdom which has learned the limits of human knowledge. It therefore approaches life with awe, hope and fear. With awe, because it knows that the mystery of life is something more than an unknown region not yet explored by an advancing science; with hope because "it doth not yet appear what we shall be" and no record of past history gives us an adequate clue of what creative omnipotence may bring forth out of the infinite possibilities of existence; with fear, because it knows the possibilities of evil, which appear at each new turn in history, are never adequately anticipated by any analysis of the past. The wisdom of such childlikeness will prefer its hopes to its fears, knowing that good is more primary than evil, that the world could not exist at all if it were not good, creation being a triumph over chaos. It will therefore approach life fearful and yet unafraid. Its serenity will be more lasting than that of a culture which based its confidence upon the illusion that human intelligence had overcome the chaos of the nature about us and the nature in us. It will not be surprised if ogres and goblins suddenly appear out of the darkness; any more than fairies and good spirits will surprise it. It knows the dimensions of life to be both deeper and higher than the thin surface of expected occurrences which has been frozen by rationalism into an icy solidity, giving those who seek a firm footing upon it a false sense of security. The ice is not very thick; the ocean beneath it is deep and tempestuous; and the sun above is warm and melting.

The relative good of every human achievement is always threatened by the chaos of evil and by the judgment of a good God who destroys man's imperfect handiwork to make room for something better. The joys of birth and the grief of death are richer, more satisfying and more terrible than the rational expectancies suggested by vital statistics. No rationalist, in the period of bourgeois complacency in which it was believed that the demonic forces in history had been permanently banned by human prudence, could have foreseen or did foresee this sorry era in the world's life, in which nations have gone mad and worship as their gods ridiculous leaders who have suddenly emerged out of the twilight zone of political burlesque.

It is not without significance that the real saints of history, as distinguished from morbid, self-flagellating ascetics, have a delightful sense of humour, as had Francis of Assisi for instance. This sense of humour is based upon a curious quality of disillusionment which has not resulted in either bitterness or despair. It is without bitterness, because judgments of the fellowman are tempered by the forgiveness which is prompted by repentance. It is without despair, because no evils in the world can disturb the firm faith in the goodness of God and his ultimate triumph over evil. This quality of mirthful serenity is unlike the innocency of childhood which knows no evil. It has looked into the abyss of evil and is no longer affrighted by it. This state might be termed a second childhood, but for the uncomplimentary connotation of that term. It is, at any rate, the spiritual state which follows the second birth of repentance and conversion.

Spiritual health in both individuals and societies is an achievement of maturity in which some excellency of childhood is consciously reclaimed, after being lost in the complexities of life. It is an inner integrity not on this but the other side of inner conflict; it is sincerity not on this but the other side of a contrite recognition of the deceitfulness of the human heart; it is trust in the goodness of life not on this but the other side of disillusionment and despair; it is naïveté and serenity not on this but the other side of sophistication. In no case is the exact outlook of the child reclaimed. What is at the end is never really like the beginning. Yet something of the beginning must be in the end, if the end is not to be pure dissolution. In both morals and culture, life and history are therefore constant battles "to become as little children," to arrest that in growth which is decay, to prevent multiciplicity from destroying unity, to prevent increased knowledge from enervating the zest for life and to prevent the atrophy of the imagination in the growth of mind.

Eight:
CHRISTIANITY
AND TRAGEDY

And there followed him a great company of people, and of women, which also bewailed and lamented him. But Jesus turning unto them said, Daughters of Jerusalem, weep not for me; but weep for yourselves and for your children.   Luke 23:27–29.

8: CHRISTIANITY AND TRAGEDY

THE WOMEN of Jerusalem wept for him. They wept for him because they loved and revered him. Perhaps they loved and revered him because they could weep for him. Pity is curiously mixed with both love and reverence. Love for equals is difficult. We love what is weak and suffers. It appeals to our strength without challenging it. But we also revere those who suffer because of their strength or nobility. If their strength is triumphant our reverence may turn into fear or even into hatred. Triumphant strength is usually mixed with force or guile. Therefore our greatest reverence is reserved for the strength which we can pity because it is too pure to be triumphant.

He did not regard his own life as pitiful. He disavowed their grief. "Weep not for me. Weep for yourselves and for your children." Jesus is, superficially considered, a tragic figure; yet not really so. Christianity is a religion which transcends tragedy. Tears, with death, are swallowed up in victory. The cross is not tragic but the resolution of tragedy. Here suffering is carried into the very life of God and overcome. It becomes the basis of salvation. Yet it has tears of pity for those who do not understand life profoundly enough to escape the chaos of impulse and chance by which most lives are determined: "Weep for yourselves and for your children."

I

This admonition "Weep for yourselves" is the recognition in the Christian view of life of what is pitiful rather than tragic in ordinary human existence. The word tragic is commonly used very loosely. It usually designates what is not tragic at all but pitiful. In true tragedy the hero defies malignant power to assert the integrity of his soul. He suffers because he is strong and not because he is weak. He involves himself in guilt not by his vice but by his virtue. This tragic level of life is an achievement of the few. Most men perish in weakness, frustration and confusion. We weep for them; but in our tears there is no catharsis of "pity and terror" such as Aristotle regards as the proof and consequence of true tragedy. There is pity but not terror. The novels of Thomas Hardy are replete with these pitiful figures. They are driven by passion and their lives are determined by circumstance. They remain weak vessels and victims of an inscrutable fate which weaves curious patterns with and into their lives. Hardy was a pessimist and his characters are therefore not tragic. Surely Nietzsche was right in his assertion, that tragedy stands beyond pessimism and optimism. Yet Hardy's characters are real enough, because so much of life is actually lived upon the level which he describes. It suffers both from frustrated and unfulfilled desires and from passions and ambitions satisfied and fulfilled at the expense of the weal of others.

Frequently our pity is the greater for such life because it does not weep for itself. It may shed tears of momentary pain. But it does not rise sufficiently above its fate to survey its meaning or to subdue the confusion out of which the pain arises. The pity is all in the spectator and not in the actor of the drama, for the spectator discerns meanings which are not beheld by the participants. In the tragedies of Ibsen our pity is usually aroused for the victims and the protagonists of unreal social conventions. They bring terrible pain upon themselves and upon each other by a sinful morality, by egotism masked behind conventional righteousness. What Ibsen describes therefore is the pathos of human sinfulness. This is true even of his most genuinely tragic figure, Brand, who suffers for his intransigeant idealism, but even more because this idealism is a screen for unconscious impulses of power. Ibsen was a realist; and perhaps realists cannot write great tragedy. In actual life pathos overwhelms tragedy and the spectator feels only pity without reverence. If there was a greater degree of comprehension in the participants of the drama of the forces which determine their action, they might be aroused to some heroic defiance of the forces and fates which enthrall them and hurl them to destruction. We weep for them because they are unable to heed the words of Jesus to the women of Jerusalem: "Weep for yourselves and for your children." This holds true of most of the so-called tragic victims of warfare. They have courage and loyalty; but both their courage and loyalty deliver them more certainly into hands of all the blind and anarchic forces which today set nation against nation. About them we could well say with Vachel Lindsay:

"Not that they serve but that they have no Gods to
   serve,
Not that they starve but that they starve so dream-
   lessly,
Not that they die but that they die like sheep."

The really tragic hero of warfare is not the soldier who makes the greatest sacrifice but the occasional discerning spirit who plunges into the chaos of war with a full understanding of its dark, unconscious sources in the human psyche and an equal resolution, either to defy these forces or to submit himself as their tool and victim in recognition of his common humanity with those who are unconscious victims.

158

II

It is not possible, of course, to comprehend all ordinary life in the category of the pitiful, and to reserve pure tragedy only for an occasional hero of great nobility and strength. The genuinely tragic is curiously compounded with the pitiful. This reveals itself whenever the victims of blind fate and chaotic impulse are enmeshed in their suffering by strength as well as by weakness, by some noble purpose as well as by blindness. Thus Othello is ensnared in a murderous jealousy by the very passion of his love for Desdemona. His strength becomes the source of his weakness. In the same way Ibsen's Peer Gynt suffers both because he is driven to and fro by every wild passion which has ever excited the human imagination and because he is moved by tremendous ambitions, too great for the human frame. Ibsen presents an even more telling picture of tragic suffering in his *Wild Duck*, in which an unimaginative wife with a spotted past bears the sorrows occasioned by the foibles of a self-righteous husband with such simple dignity and patience that her sufferings are transmuted from the pitiful to the tragic. In this class of semi-tragic figures we must also place Shakespeare's King Lear, who is the victim of both his love and his obtuseness so that he loves the daughters who hate him and hates the daughter who loves him.

These figures of literature all mirror a real aspect of human existence. This aspect is revealed whenever men suffer not because of their strength but manifest such strength and dignity in their suffering that the pitiful is lifted into a nobler category and weakness is transmuted into sublimity. In this category we may also count those who suffer wrongs guiltlessly, not because of any brave defiance of established evil but simply because they are bound together in the same bundle of life with the guilty, mothers suffering for erring children or wives for wayward husbands, and transmuting the pain by some achievement of serenity or imagination so that it ceases to be a natural fate and becomes a spiritual triumph.

This type of suffering does not yet introduce us to the purest tragedy. In pure tragedy the suffering is self-inflicted. The hero does not transmute what happens to him but initiates the suffering by his own act. For the purest conception of tragedy we turn to the Greek drama, particularly the drama of Æschylos and Sophocles. The hero of Greek tragedy suffers either because he defies God or because he is forced to violate some code of historical morality in the name of what seems to him a higher duty. He perishes because of his very strength. In the Promethean myth the hero is not a man at all but a demi-god who defies Zeus for the sake of endowing mankind with all the arts. In this myth we come very close to the Christian

conception of the inevitable guilt of pride which at-
taches to the highest human enterprise. Man becomes
guilty of "hybris" and arouses the jealousy of God.
But since God is conceived as only just and not loving
he is something less than just. He is vindictive. The
Promethean tragedy, in other words, recognises the
perennial self-destruction of man by his overreaching
himself. But it sees no solution for the problem.
Æschylos, indeed, suggests again and again that men
must observe the law of measure, thus introducing
the solution of prudence, which became the very
foundation of Aristotelian ethics. But the heroes of
Æschylos are tragically noble precisely because they
disregard the author's pious advice.

The Æschylian plot is more profound than the
Æschylian philosophy; for it recognises that man is
endowed not only with a rational faculty which seeks
to bring all things into orderly relation with each
other but with an imagination which surveys the
heavens, aspires to the stars and breaks all the little
systems of prudence which the mind constructs. It is
this imagination which is the root of all human creativity; but also the source of all human evil. The
closer Greek tragedy remains to its source of Dionysic
myth the more it expresses this titanic defiance of
rational morality; for the myth embodies an unconscious penetration into the heart of life which Greek
philosophers never knew. The philosophers con-

structed systems of justice, even as our moral philosophers do, which would have destroyed both good and evil if any one had observed them. The tragic poet could not get beyond the conception that evil was inextricably involved in the most creative forces of human life. From the standpoint of his conception life was therefore purely tragic. It destroyed itself in its noblest bursts of creativity, which always broke the limits placed upon human effort by divine jealousy.

The Promethean motif is, however, not a dominant, though a perpetual, note in Greek tragedy. It is clearly expressed only in the tragedy of that name. In most of the other tragedies of Æschylos and Sophocles, the tragedy arises from the hero's conscious affirmation of unconscious human impulses in defiance of society's conventions, not to say of society's necessary schemes of morality. Agamemnon thus kills his daughter, Iphigenia, in order to insure success to his martial enterprise, offering her as a sacrifice to the gods. Clytemnestra murders Agamemnon in order to avenge her daughter. Orestes kills his mother to avenge his father. Sometimes, as in the case of Œdipus, a crime is committed unknowingly; for he murders his father and marries his mother inadvertently. On the whole the emphasis is not on inadvertent guilt, however, but upon a guilt with which the hero covers himself because he affirms some primitive, powerful and partly unconscious passion of the soul in defiance of the moral law. The human will is made the door into action of all those dark and turgid but also sublime and noble impulses which lie below the level of human consciousness. In what is probably the profoundest of the tragedies of Æschylos, *The Eumenides*, Orestes' matricide is carefully analysed. It is proved that the deed was committed at the behest of Apollo and he is justified in it by the goddess Athena. Yet is he hounded by the avenging furies. He had not only broken a convention of society. He had actually committed a wrong. He had murdered his mother. Yet piety toward the memory of his father had prompted the act; and this piety is conceived as an inspiration of Apollo.

The tragic motif in Greek drama is thus either Promethean or Dionysian (Freudian). In the one case the human imagination breaks the forms of prudent morality because it strives toward the infinite; in the other because it expresses passions and impulses which lie below the level of consciousness in ordinary men and which result in consequences outside the bounds of decent morality. The Greek drama thus surveys the heights and depths of the human spirit and uncovers a total dimension which prudence can neither fully comprehend nor restrain. But the tragic hero is not a mere victim of these passions and ambitions. He wilfully affirms in his own act what may be an unconscious impulse or an inscrutable necessity in lesser men. In that sense Greek tragedy is both romantic and aristocratic: romantic because it affirms the whole of life, whatever the consequences, in its dimension of nature and infinity, of Dionysian impulse and Promethean will; aristocratic because only a few titans and heroes dare to break the bounds which check ordinary men. Greek tragedy declares that the vitality of life is in conflict with the laws of life. It does not draw pessimistic or negative conclusions from this fact. The tragic hero simply undertakes to break the laws in order to express the full dimension of human existence. The tragic hero is an aristocrat for precisely the opposite reason of Aristotle's and Plato's aristocrat, who expresses his superiority over lesser men by the restraint which reason has placed upon emotion.

One weakness of the tragic hero is that he is always crying "Weep for me." He needs a chorus to extol his virtues and justify his actions. He requires lesser men to appreciate his true greatness. There is in other words an inevitable element of self-pity in classic tragedy. Matthew Arnold expresses this element in the final lines of his poem, "The Last Word":

> "Charge once more then and be dumb.
> Let the victors when they come,
> When the forts of folly fall,
> Find thy body by the wall."

What would the hero of tragedy do without these weeping, appreciating and revering spectators? This necessity of pity from the lesser men who keep the law for the greater men who break it out of an inner necessity is the symbol of an unresolved conflict in the heart of Greek tragedy. It does not know where the real centre of life lies, whether in its law or in its vitality. Therefore the weak law-abiders must honour the strong law-breakers, lest the latter seem dishonourable.

III

However wide and deep the differences which separate the Christian view of life from that of Greek tragedy, it must be apparent that there are greater similarities between the two than between either and the utilitarian rationalism which has dominated contemporary culture. Both measure life in the same depth; and neither gives itself to the simple delusion that the titanic forces of human existence, whether they spring from below the level of consciousness or rise above the level of human limitations, can easily be brought under the control of some little scheme of prudent rationality.

Christianity and Greek tragedy agree that guilt and creativity are inextricably interwoven. But Christianity does not regard the inevitability of guilt in all human creativity as inherent in the nature of human life. Sin emerges, indeed, out of freedom and is possible only because man is free; but it is done in freedom, and therefore man and not life bears responsibility for it. It does indeed accompany every creative act; but the evil is not part of the creativity. It is the consequence of man's self-centredness and egotism by which he destroys the harmony of existence. The fact that he does this is not an occasion for admiration but for pity: "Weep for yourselves" remains Christianity's admonition to all who involve themselves in sin and guilt, whether by unconscious submission to forces greater than their will or by consciously affirming these forces.

A survey of the modern titans and heroes, whether nations or the oligarchs of nations, whether political or economic and industrial oligarchs, must certainly justify this Christian estimate of their true character. These nations and these leaders overreach themselves so pitifully. Their strength is so obviously bogus. It is weakness which poses as strength; it is the pride of an inferiority complex. It may create but it destroys more than it creates. It involves Europe in carnage for the sake of a brief hour of glory. Like Agamemnon, it sacrifices its Iphigenia under the illusion that the father who sacrifices a daughter, the nation which sacrifices its sons, for the sake of victory, is proving its unselfishness. It forgets, like Agamemnon, that the pride of the man and not the unselfishness of the father is the dominant motif in the sacrifice.

It must be admitted, of course, that there are genuinely tragic elements in the human enterprise, simply because nobility and strength, dignity and creative ambition are mixed with this sin, and frequently make it more destructive. Thus Japan lives in greater ultimate insecurity than China because Japanese patriotism has created a nation of greater unity and force than China, a nation playing for higher stakes, at greater risks and with the certainty of ultimate disaster. In the same way the British Empire could not have been built without the solid achievements of British statecraft, a statecraft which made moral qualities serve political purposes. But the British aristocrats who built the Empire are also sealing its doom by policies which are prompted by some of the same class characteristics which were responsible for their original success. However we may qualify the judgment to allow for authentic tragic elements in human life, Christianity is right in its general indictment, "Weep for yourselves." Sin is pitiful.

The Saviour who utters these words dies upon the cross. He dies not because he has sinned but because he has not sinned. He proves thereby that sin is so much a part of existence that sinlessness cannot maintain itself in it. But he also proves that sin is not a

167

necessary and inherent characteristic of life. Evil is
not a part of God, nor yet a part of essential man.
This Saviour is a revelation of the goodness of God
and the essential goodness of man, *i.e.,* the second
Adam. He is indeed defeated in history but in that
very defeat proves that he cannot be ultimately
defeated. That is, he reveals that it is God's nature
to swallow up evil in Himself and destroy it. Life in
its deepest essence is not only good but capable of
destroying the evil which has been produced in it.
Life is thus not at war with itself. Its energy is not
in conflict with its order. Hence the Saviour truly
says: "Weep not for me." Christianity stands beyond
tragedy. If there are tears for this man on the cross
they cannot be tears of "pity and terror." The cross
does not reveal life at cross purposes with itself. On
the contrary, it declares that what seems to be an
inherent defect in life itself is really a contingent
defect in the soul of each man, the defect of the sin
which he commits in his freedom. If he can realise
that fact, if he can weep for himself, if he can repent,
he can also be saved. He can be saved by hope and
faith. His hope and faith will separate the character
of life in its essential reality from life as it is revealed
in sinful history.

This man on the cross who can say "Weep not for
me" is also able to save us from our tears of self-pity.
What he reveals about life transmutes tears of self-

pity into tears of remorse and repentance. Repentance does not accuse life or God but accuses self. In that self-accusation lies the beginning of hope and salvation. If the defect lies in us and not in the character of life, life is not hopeless. If we can only weep for ourselves as men we need not weep for ourselves as man.

Nine:
THE SUFFERING
SERVANT AND THE
SON OF MAN

When Jesus came into the coasts of Cæsarea Philippi, he asked his disciples, saying, Whom do men say that I, the Son of man, am? And they said, Some say that thou art John the Baptist: some Elias; and others, Jeremias, or one of the prophets. He saith unto them, But whom say ye that I am? And Simon Peter answered and said, Thou art the Christ, the Son of the living God.

And Jesus answered and said unto him, Blessed art thou, Simon Barjona: for flesh and blood hath not revealed it unto thee, but my Father which is in heaven. And I say also unto thee, That thou art Peter, and upon this rock I will build my church; and the gates of hell shall not prevail against it. And I will give unto thee the keys of the kingdom of heaven: and whatsoever thou shalt bind on earth, shall be bound in heaven: and whatsoever thou shalt loose on earth, shall be loosed in heaven.

Then charged he his disciples that they should tell no man that he was Jesus the Christ. From that time forth began Jesus to shew unto his disciples, how that he must go unto Jerusalem, and suffer many things of the elders and chief priests and scribes, and be killed, and be raised again the third day. Then Peter took him, and began to rebuke him, saying, Be it far from thee, Lord: this shall not be unto thee. But he turned, and said unto Peter, Get thee behind me, Satan: thou art an offence unto me: for thou savourest not the things that be of God, but those that be of men.

Then said Jesus unto his disciples, If any man will come after me, let him deny himself, and take up his cross, and follow me. For whosoever will save his life shall lose it: and whosoever will lose his life for my sake shall find it. For what is a man profited, if he shall gain the whole world, and lose his own soul? or what shall a man give in exchange for his soul? For the Son of man shall come in the glory of his Father, with his angels; and then he shall reward every man according to his works. Verily I say unto you, There be some standing here, which shall not taste of death, till they see the Son of man coming in his kingdom.

Matthew 16:13–28.

9: THE SUFFERING SERVANT AND THE SON OF MAN

You are the Christ," answered Peter to Jesus' question. "That confession of faith," said Jesus, "is more true than you could realise. You are the mouthpiece of God in making it. But even now I doubt whether you understand what it means to be the Messiah. We will go to Jerusalem where I must suffer and die." "Lord," said Peter, "you must not allow that to happen. Certainly it is not the destiny of God's messenger to suffer but to triumph." "Now you are the mouthpiece of Satan," said Jesus, probably leaving Peter a little confused and embarrassed to be regarded in the course of a few moments as both God's and Satan's tool. Peter was the mouthpiece of Satan for being only half wrong and yet very wrong. The Messiah would triumph in the end. First the Messiah must suffer and die and be raised up and then he would come again "in all his glory." Peter understood the triumph but not the relation of suffering to it.

I

If we are to understand the implications of this conversation between Jesus and Peter it is necessary, briefly, to review the various Messianic ideas which were current in Jesus' day. One of them was the idea that the Messiah would be a second David, a great king, who would reign through his power and goodness. One might designate this idea, without unfairness, as political messianism. Jesus had rejected it in the experience of the wilderness, where it came to him as the temptation to rule over all the kingdoms of the world. It is significant that he rejected it then in words strangely similar to those which startled the hapless Peter: "Get thee behind me, Satan." Jesus must have felt very strongly that this political conception of the Messianic rule was a temptation. Another, more popular, conception of the Messianic reign was the apocalyptic one, to be found in Daniel and in the Fourth Ezra and other apocalyptic literature. The Messiah would be a man from heaven, a transcendent messenger at whose coming the whole world order would be transmuted. Nature itself would be transformed. The "good time" of earlier Messianic hopes became, in this view, the "end of time." The name for this man from heaven was "the son of a man," a name which Jesus appropriated for himself.

There was a third conception, not at all popular among those who pondered on the future. It was the idea of the "suffering servant" in the fifty-third chapter of Isaiah. Undoubtedly the prophet used the idea for the whole of Israel rather than for any particular person. It did not belong to the popular conceptions. Quite obviously Jesus arrived at his conception of the Messianic reign by rejecting the first idea and combining the other two. They are combined not only in this conversation with Peter but in the well-known phrase "The son of man must suffer." Whether Peter was thinking in terms of the political or the apocalyptic idea we do not know. He certainly failed to think of the idea of the suffering servant. It is interesting that in Jesus' rebuke he is told that he thinks about these things like a man and not like God. Peter is thus in the position of being regarded a mouthpiece of Satan for applying human standards to ultimate and divine problems.

It might be profitable to consider the implications of such a judgment further, but let us return to the point: Jesus arrived at his definition of the Messianic reign, which he was to initiate by rejecting the political hope of a Messiah who would be a powerful and yet perfectly good king. Instead he believed that it would have to be ushered in by pure goodness which had no power. But pure goodness, without power, cannot maintain itself in the world. It ends on

177

the cross. Yet that is not where it finally ends. The
Messiah will finally transmute the whole world
order. The contradictions of human existence which
prevent power from ever being good enough to belong to the Kingdom and which equally prevent pure
love from being powerful enough to establish itself
in the world, must be finally overcome; but they can
only be overcome by divine action. No human action,
proceeding from these contradictions, is equal to it.
Here is the simple thesis of the Lord's messianism.
To understand it more fully we ought to look again
at all three terms in his equation.

II

The political idea rejected by Jesus was older than
Hebrew prophecy. There are suggestions of it in both
Egyptian and Babylonian life and history. The ideal
world would come with an ideal king, who would use
his tremendous power for purely ideal ends. Perhaps
Plato's philosopher-king is merely a rationalised version of this old hope of the ideal king, who "would
not break the bruised reed," who would "judge with
equity the meek," whose justice would rise in its
insight to imaginative love, for he would not judge
"according to the seeing of the eye or the hearing
of the ear." The ninth and eleventh chapters of
Isaiah contain classic statements of this hope. Perhaps
it ought to be mentioned that even in this political

hope a transcendent element appears. A king as good as that would have to be sent by God. As early as the messianism of Egypt we have the conception that Re himself, the sun god of Egypt, would come to the world as such a king.

If we analyse the unavailability of this political hope we may arrive at a fairly general principle of criticism for all political utopianism. The trouble with the idea is that all power in human history is too partial to be good. Hosea was the first prophet to see this. "Where," said he, "is the king who will bring prosperity to all your cities?" If Hitler is really the divine ruler the Germans imagine, he will hardly seem to be divine to the nations at whose expense Germany would triumph. This is as true of power in the life of a single nation as the use of power between nations. The power which organises society is wielded by a particular group; and inasfar as it rests upon that group it will not be as unequivocally interested in the general welfare as it claims to be. The communists think they have eliminated this partiality of power in a classless society in which the dictatorship affirms the interests of all except those who oppose the general welfare. But the Moscow trials have demonstrated how quickly the cruel facts of history refute these utopian dreams. It was to cover this hiatus between dreams and reality that the Russian dictatorship was under the fateful compulsion of proving that Trotzky, who challenged the ruling oligarchy, was really a fascist. Politics is always a contest of power. At its best it arrives at a tentative equilibrium of power. "The peace of the world," said Augustine, "is based on strife." There may be long periods of covert rather than overt struggle. But this is not the love and harmony of the Kingdom of God. Perhaps Jesus regarded the political aspect of messianism as such a terrible temptation because illusions about politics lead to the most baneful consequences. They lead to the religious sanctification of the inevitable injustices of a particular power. Thus Russia, in spite of its great achievements, is a partial return to the political strategy of Babylonian and Egyptian priest-kings who claimed unqualified religious sanctity for the very relative justice of their rule.

It does not follow that, because the balances of power, by which justice is achieved in the collective life of man, do not belong to the Kingdom of God, we are therefore to have nothing to do with them. We live in a world in which the Kingdom is not established, in which the fate of the King of love is crucifixion. In large areas of life our concern must therefore be to prevent life from destroying life. This problem of elementary justice can be solved neither by returning to the ideal of the good king nor by trying to introduce pure goodness without power into the world. Mr. Frank Buchman and the Oxford Groups have stumbled on the first idea. They dream of the Kingdom of God on earth through the conversion of Henry Ford or Adolf Hitler. Pacifism and other forms of absolutism try to apply the second idea. They regard the ideal of pure goodness without power as a simple moral possibility which waits for its application only upon a resolute moral decision. They do not understand the sinful contradictions in human nature; and do not see that even the man who tries to live in terms of pure love will display qualities of selfishness in his life from which other men must be protected. No sinful man, even when he understands that the law of life is love, can be trusted completely to be just, if his egotism does not meet resistance. We are still living in a world which falls short of the Kingdom of God even though the law of the Kingdom has been revealed to it.

III

In order to understand that fact more fully it is necessary to analyse the implications of the idea of the suffering servant. The suffering servant does not impose goodness upon the world by his power. Rather he suffers, being powerless, from the injustices of the powerful. He suffers most particularly from the sins of the righteous who do not understand how full of unrighteousness is all human righteousness.

The Saviour of the world is not crucified by criminals or obviously evil people; he is crucified with criminals by the "princes of this world," to use the Pauline phrase. Love is the law of life; but when it enters the world of relative justice and balanced egotism it is destroyed in it. The suffering servant dies on the cross. This paradox is perfectly expressed in the Johannine Gospel: "He was in the world and the world was made through him . . . he came unto his own and his own received him not." The implication is that human nature has deviated from the law of its existence, that man is estranged from his essential nature. Christ is the essential nature of man, or as St. Paul expresses it, the "second Adam." But the second Adam is not a simple moral possibility for sinful human nature, as the liberal church has believed. The second Adam is crucified by the first Adam, particularly by the first Adam who is trying to be good and is seeking to build up governments and churches and standards of conduct which will hold sin in check. Jesus is destroyed by the chief priests and elders, the princes of the world; and his chief opponents are the best people of his day, the Pharisees.

Thus when the Kingdom of God enters the world it is judged by the world and found to be dangerous to all of its tentative harmonies and relative justice. But it also judges the world in the very moment

in which the world is condemning it. The commandment of love which Christ introduces in the world
was "from the beginning," the life which he manifests
is the very pattern of life. The world does not know
how far it has strayed from that pattern until the
original is revealed. Thus Jesus declares in a Johannine
passage which expresses the meaning of the gospel
if not the exact words of Jesus: "If I had not come
and spoken unto them they had not had sin, but now
they have no cloke for their sin" (John 15:22). The
sinful world is not destroyed by the Kingdom of God.
It is however fully revealed. Any one who really
understands the dimension of the Kingdom of God
ceases to have illusions about the world's kingdoms.
He knows that their power and the relative justice of
their balances of power are not the Kingdom of God.
He knows that the anarchy of sin is still in them. If
he tries to mitigate the anarchy by relative righteousness he will not regard that righteousness as the
righteousness of the Kingdom of God. The righteousness of the Kingdom of God stands above it and
condemns it. Without the acceptance of that judgment, that is, without repentance, there is no entrance
into the Kingdom of God. For without such repentance men live in the world without knowing that
the goodness of the world is filled with evil and that
the order and peace of the world are only an armistice
between competitive forces. Without repentance those

183

who have created peace through their power imagine that they have created pure peace; and suffer from the delusion that the enemies of their peace are God's enemies. Without repentance the princes of the world, whether priests or governors, crucify the Lord afresh.

But what if the King and the Kingdom are accepted? What if the law of life is understood? Can a man then simply live by it? The modern church has usually given a simple affirmative to that question. Its answer betrays that it has forgotten that the Kingdom of God enters the world in tragic terms. The "prince of glory" dies on the cross. The modern church has, in other words, repeated Peter's mistake. The whole confusion of modern Christianity could in fact be judged in terms of Jesus' contrasting judgment upon Peter. "You understand, Peter, and are the mouthpiece of God.—You don't understand, Peter, and are the instrument of the devil." The simple moralism of the modern church is a corruption of the idea of the Kingdom in the very moment of its deepest insight into it. Its mistake is to believe that the law of love will simply prevail in the world; that it requires only resolute action by good men. It believes that if you are forgiving toward your foe, your foe will relent. But your foe may take advantage of your forgiving spirit. (Has not the white man taken advantage of the forgiving spirit of the Negro?) It believes that if only a modern nation were adventurous enough not to arm and defend itself against its foes it would shame its foes into goodness. But a defenseless Germany after the war was driven to madness by the vindictiveness of its foes. Now these foes are arming frantically to keep pace with the arms of vindictive Germany. Human sin always involves itself in these vicious circles. They are so obviously vicious that good men, who do not understand the depth of human sinfulness, always imagine that sin will reduce itself to an absurdity and allow the strategy of the Kingdom a clear field. Unfortunately, there is nothing in human history to substantiate this hope.

The Kingdom of God must still enter the world by way of the crucifixion. Goodness, armed with power, is corrupted; and pure love without power is destroyed. If it succeeds occasionally, as it does, it gives us vital and creative symbols of the fact that the Kingdom of God is a reality as well as a possibility. But if any one trusts himself to it only as an established reality he will be disappointed. "Rejoice not that the devils are subject unto you," said Jesus, "but that your name is recorded in heaven." If you rejoice that you can actually conquer evil you will hazard an action only if you are certain of triumph. Thus every morality which begins by counting on the success of a pure action must end by reducing the purity of the action in the interest of its success. The whole moral con-

185

fusion of the church in regard to philanthropy is a consequence of such logic. Philanthropy is usually a generous concession of power to weakness. It usually does not touch the equilibrium of social power and it is therefore something less than justice. It becomes corrupted into an enemy of justice as soon as the next step is taken and it is used by the powerful to beguile the weak from challenging the basic equilibrium of justice. Thus every easy assurance of triumph for the Kingdom of God falsifies the human situation and beguiles men into false conceptions of the tragedy of human history. Where success is the unintended rather than intended consequence of an action oriented in the cross it becomes a symbol of the second coming, a reminder that the Kingdom is not ultimately defeated, though it is immediately defeated.

Through all the ages of Christian history there have been faithful spirits who sought to cut through all the relativities of life and to live purely by the principles of Christ. Catholic monastics have on the whole understood the problems involved in this enterprise better than modern liberal Christians. They remained celibate and assumed no responsibility for establishing the relative standards of justice without which the world cannot live. They understood that such responsibilities inevitably involved one in the defense of one family against other families and one nation against other nations. Perhaps they did not understand sufficiently to what degree the ascetic is a parasite on the sins of his fellowmen and that he ought therefore to claim no moral advantage over them. If he does understand that and escapes the sin of Pharisaism, he may become a valuable reminder to the Christian community of the fact that the Kingdom of God has come and that its law is the law of life, even though men cannot maintain themselves in the world of sin by obedience to it.

IV

The discussion thus far brings us to the conclusion that there is no final escape in historic existence from the contradictions in which human nature is involved, from the fact that "there is a law in our members which wars against the law that is in our minds." This naturally introduces us to the final element in Jesus' conception of the Kingdom of God. He regarded himself not only as the suffering servant but as the "son of man." The historic conception of the son of man was that he was a "man from heaven" who had been from the beginning and would at the end introduce into the world the pattern of life from which it had strayed. But the apocalyptic writers were quite clear that this final consummation involved a transmutation of the whole world order. This new world would not be some "eternal life" of Greek conception but a transmuted temporal order. In trying to portray this new world order symbols of both temporality and eternity appear. Men would live to be a thousand years and yet never grow old; yet the righteous of the past would be resurrected.

So fantastic are some of these concepts that rationalists have made them the object of their scorn while millenarian sects have revelled in the luxuriant fantasies of Daniel and the book of Revelation, intent upon proving some cryptic symbol to be a proof of their particular hopes and prejudices. Yet the idea of a second coming of the Messiah (and of the coming of a transcendent Messiah in the pre-Christian apocalypses) contains some of the most basic paradoxes of the Christian religion. The two most basic ideas in this hope of the "parousia" are that the redemption of the world does not require the destruction of creation since creation is not of itself evil, and secondly that redemption must come from God since every human action remains with the contradictions of sin.

The first idea can be expressed only in terms of a chronological myth. This inevitably leads to illusions, as all myths do. In this case it leads to chronological illusions about the end of the world. But as in all true myths its concept cannot be expressed in purely rational terms. Salvation lies at the end of history and not in some realm of eternity above history, because Christianity, in common with prophetic thought, does not regard creation as evil, does not believe that

particularisation or individualisation is the beginning of anarchy. Stated in simpler terms it does
not believe that man is an egotist because he is an ego.
Sin arises out of man's freedom and not out of his
individuality. There is therefore an ideal possibility
that individuals, though free, would be so related to
the divine centre of existence, that they would not
usurp a larger place for themselves than is their due.
But this ideal possibility is not realised. Man is a
sinner who disturbs the harmony of existence. This
sin is an inevitability from which man cannot free
himself. If God frees him of it, this salvation does
not involve the destruction of all temporal and individual reality. The Kingdom of God is in that
sense in history.

This symbol Christianity must maintain against
both dualistic and mystic religions. By this symbol it
declares that historic existence is not meaningless, in
spite of the corruption of sin within it, and in spite of
the fact that it points to an unconditioned good which
is not realised in any known history. History may
defeat the Christ but it nevertheless points to him as
the law of life. Thus every deed of love points to an
ultimate triumph in the very hour of its defeat, just
as Christ himself sees before him both the cross and
the son of man "coming in all his glory and all his
holy angels with him." The Christ who is obedient
even unto death is not only highly exalted to sit at

the right hand of God but "he will come again."

It is interesting how the chiliastic sects of the Reformation period used these symbols of the second coming (not without chronological and utopian illusions) to express the idea of a meaningful history against a pessimistic and individualistic Protestantism which had become, in effect, a neo-platonic dualism. Mankind does not destroy the law of life by violating it. It operates in history, if in no other way than by destroying those who violate it. Every empire which seeks to make itself the centre and law of existence is ultimately destroyed. Nor is mankind ever totally depraved. Total depravity is an impossibility, since man can be a sinner only because he is a child of God. He can do evil only because he has freedom; and freedom is the mark of his divine sonship. It is therefore impossible to express the Christian idea of salvation in purely rational terms, for they suggest that temporal existence is, by its very temporality, a corruption of ultimate reality. The pattern of life is not corrupted by historic existence but in historic existence. Thus the Kingdom of God must come in history.

Yet when it comes, it is the end of history. Ultimate salvation is not a moral possibility. The sinful self-contradiction in the human spirit cannot be overcome by moral action, since every moral action, even the highest and purest, expresses it. The world cannot live by the laws of Christ, not only because (as Luther put it) there are not enough Christians but because no one is Christlike enough. Human society may continue to develop from primitive innocency to maturity; but there is no final conquest of good over evil in this development. Both good and evil develop. Both the city of God and the city of the world grow, as Augustine observed. History consequently presents a problem which points beyond history. Suggestions of this idea begin to appear in the earliest prophecies of the Kingdom of God, even before apocalyptic seers develop the logic inherent in these suggestions to its final conclusion. Even the ideal king of political messianism is to come from God; and in his reign the lion will lie down with the lamb, *i.e.*, nature itself will be transmuted.

If Christianity, when true to its prophetic heritage, sets the symbol of a Kingdom of God in history against mystical and rational otherworldliness, it must likewise set the symbol of the end of history against all naturalistic utopianism. It is the particular weakness of naturalism to disavow the eternal ground of history and imagine that the course of temporal events is self-explanatory and self-containing and then, curiously and inconsistently, to hope for the appearance of an unconditioned good in history. The liberal utopians expect such a utopia when reason has overcome the impulses of nature; and the Marxian utopians expect it when a classless society has destroyed the conflict between classes. In each case the seriousness of human sin is not understood. The liberal does not understand that mind may sharpen as well as compose the conflict of life with life. The Marxian does not see that the injustices of capitalist society are but one form, or perhaps one consequence, of man's sinful defiance of the law of love. The Marxian is right in looking forward to a higher justice, based upon the socialisation of property, for to socialise property means to create a higher equilibrium of power in a world now rushing to destruction because of the peculiarly dangerous disproportions of economic power in a technical society. But he is wrong if he imagines that this new equilibrium of power will so change human nature as to do away with the necessity of power and thus usher in an anarchistic millennium.

The Kingdom of God thus lies beyond history. But the Kingdom of God is not some realm of eternity which negates time. It is a realm of eternity which fulfils time. Therefore it is not impossible for the eternal to set up a symbol in time. That is Christ and the Kingdom of the suffering servant. But it is also possible that the defeat of this suffering servant should have within itself the symbol of an ultimate victory. The basic plan of life cannot be finally defeated. The will of God prevails even when the Son of God is crucified. In that very crucifixion God has absorbed the contradictions of historic existence into Himself. Thus Christianity transmutes the tragedy of history into something which is not tragedy. God is revealed as not only the ground but as the goal of human existence and man's rebellion against God is proved to be an abortive effort which cannot finally prevail. The suffering servant is the son of man.

This is the foolishness of God that is wiser than the wisdom of men.

Ten:
TRANSVALUATION
OF VALUES

For ye see your calling, brethren, how that not many wise men after the flesh, not many mighty, not many noble, are called. But God hath chosen the foolish things of the world to confound the wise; and God hath chosen the weak things of the world to confound the things which are mighty; And base things of the world, and things which are despised, hath God chosen, yea, and things which are not, to bring to nought things that are: That no flesh should glory in his presence.

I Corinthians 1:26–29.

10: TRANSVALUATION OF VALUES

I

THE APOSTLE Paul could hardly have given Nietzsche's quarrel with Christianity a clearer justification than we find in these uncompromising words. Christianity, declared Nietzsche, is the vengeance the slaves have taken upon their masters. Driven by resentment, "a resentment experienced by creatures who, deprived as they are of the proper outlet of action, are forced to find their compensation in imaginary revenge," they have transvalued the morality of the aristocrats and have turned sweet into bitter and bitter into sweet.

Nietzsche is quite right. Christianity does transvalue historical values. In human history wealth, fame and immortality are given to the wise, the mighty and the noble. They receive the plaudits of their fellowmen in their lifetime; and their names are recorded on monuments and in historical chronicles so that they may not perish in the memories of those who come after them. Their bodies are fed by the toil of their fellows and the pride of their souls is sustained by the adulation, respect, fear and even resentment of those whom they bestride.

Yet St. Paul dares to declare that in the Kingdom of God not many of the great of the world will be chosen. He does not exclude them. "Not many are called," is his measured phrase. One is reminded of Jesus' simile of the rich man and the eye of the needle. The rich man's salvation is impossible for man, yet "with God all things are possible." These words of Paul are really a neat and succinct summary of a general biblical emphasis. Amos pronounced judgment upon those who "lie upon beds of ivory and stretch themselves upon their couches, that eat the lambs out of the flock—and anoint themselves with the chief ointments, but they are not grieved for the affliction of Joseph." The Magnificat of Mary is in the same spirit: "He hath put down the mighty from their seats, and exalted them to low degree. He hath filled the hungry with good things; and the rich he hath sent empty away." The words of Jesus are filled with similar suggestions of the transvaluation of the hierarchies of history in the Kingdom of God. The story of Dives and Lazarus is unmistakable in its meaning. The Parable of the Labourers in the Vineyard closes with the words, "So the last shall be first and the first last; for many are called but few are chosen." In the Beatitudes he pronounces blessings upon the poor in spirit. In the Lukan version this is rendered, "Blessed be ye poor," and the logic of transvaluation is completed with the corollary, "Woe unto you that are rich! . . . Woe unto you that are full." There is no real contradiction between Matthew's and Luke's version; for in all probability they are merely different renderings of the Hebrew *amha—ares*, the "poor of the land," a phrase which includes the connotation of humility as well as of poverty. It is in fact this double connotation which gives a clue to the whole meaning of the gospel's transvaluation of values.

The mighty, the rich and the noble are condemned precisely because their position tempts them to a pride which is offensive in the sight of God. Thus Isaiah declares: "Woe to the crown of pride, to the drunkards of Ephraim, whose glorious beauty is a fading flower. . . . The crown of pride, the drunkards of Ephraim shall be trodden under foot." Nietzsche is quite right. The whole of biblical thought is charged with anti-aristocratic ideas, with hopes and predictions that in God's sight the estimates which history places upon human achievements will be overturned.

II

The question is, Was Nietzsche right in his belief that this transvaluation of values represented a threat to all the highest values of human culture? Was he

justified in his lament, "Everything is obviously becoming Judaised, or Christianised or vulgarised—it
seems impossible to stop this poisoning through the
whole body politic of mankind"?

The answer is that if history should itself turn
over its own values and periodically cast the mighty
from their seats and exalt them of low degree, this
would happen only because history is forced partly
to validate, though it usually defies, the standards of
the Kingdom of God. History is nature; and in nature
the strong devour the weak and the shrewd take
advantage of the simple. But human history is more
than nature. It is a realm of freedom where the
inequalities of nature are accentuated by human
imagination until they become intolerable and destroy
themselves. Thus the ultimate religious judgments
upon the strong and the weak, the proud and the
humble, are always momentarily defied with impunity, but ultimately validated in history.

Let us consider the various classes of eminence in
order: "Not many mighty after the flesh are called."
To begin with the mighty changes St. Paul's order
for the sake of bringing the most obvious group to
judgment first. Not many mighty are called. They
are certainly called in the kingdoms of the world;
and rightly so. The mighty are very necessary to the
kingdoms of the world. They organise society. The
first larger social units, the empires, which gradually

coalesced out of the earlier city-states and clans, are the handiwork of the mighty. Empires are built by the prowess of warriors and the guile of priests. The part which priests played in the building of early civilisations must warn us not to identify force with might, *i.e.*, to interpret might in purely physical terms. Societies are organised by those who hold the most significant social power of the moment, whether it be religious influence, military force or economic ownership. This function of the mighty in society is necessary and indispensable; so indispensable, that many national societies achieved unity only through a foreign conqueror.

Yet the mighty stand under the judgment of God in a special sense. They are, of all men, most tempted to transgress the bounds of human creatureliness and to imagine themselves God. The degree to which the mighty have deified themselves from the days of the earliest priest-kings and god-kings to the contemporary Hitler is an illuminating indication of the temptation to which the mighty invariably succumb. The perennial sin of man is his rebellion against God, his inclination to make himself God. All men are tempted to this sin; but the mighty are particularly subject to it. In an interesting book of Wall Street gossip entitled *They Told Barron*, published some years ago, the story is told of a man who came with a wry face, from an interview with one of America's financial overlords, and explained his discomfiture with the words, "I have just been subjected to the unconscious arrogance of conscious power." The religious prophet sees this arrogance of the mighty as primarily a sin against God. The mighty man is incapable of the humility which all sinful men should have before God. Consequently God will assert his power over them. Therefore Isaiah prophesies that "The crown of pride, the drunkards of Ephraim shall be trodden under foot," and "in that day shall the Lord of hosts be for a crown of glory and a diadem of beauty, unto the residue of his people."

But this judgment of God is executed not only at the end of history. It is executed periodically in history. The mighty men sin against men as well as God. The expanding self of mighty men grows too tall and affronts God. But wherever life exceeds its just bounds it also grows too broad and destroys other life near it. The mighty men are like tall trees whose branches rob neighbouring trees of the sunshine they require for their life. In other words, the social sin of the mighty is that they demand too high a price from society for the services they render. They not only demand it but get it. They get it because they control the organs by which society comes to self-consciousness and thinks and acts. Whether the mighty men are priestly rulers, military chieftains or economic overlords they always become involved in the same self-destructive process. At first they create social peace and a modicum of justice by their power. Then they disturb social peace and destroy justice by the exactions of their power. They involve society in internal strife by demanding exorbitant rewards for the service they render; also they involve it in external strife by using their control of their fellow men for the satisfaction of their imperial ambitions beyond the borders of their own social system. Thus injustice is the social consequence of pride; and the inevitable fruit of injustice is self-destruction.

In Egon Friedell's *A Cultural History of the Modern Age* this self-destroying inclination of all oligarchies is succinctly expressed in the following words: "In every state there is but one single class that rules, and this means that it rules illegally. It is darkly conscious of this—and it seeks to justify it by clearer dialectic and fiery declamation, to soften it by brilliant deeds and merits, by private integrity, by mildness in practice; not seldom it even suffers under it. But it cannot help itself. . . . Deep-rooted in human beings, this heart's inertia, this spiritual cowardice that never dares to acknowledge its own wrongdoing is the secret malady of which all societies perish. . . . It is the common abyss that will swallow Liberalism, Clericalism, plutocracy and proletarian dictatorship. Salvation from the curse of injustice is possible only in a Christian state but such a state has never existed."

This interesting historical observation could be put in another way, as follows: Every human society ultimately transgresses the laws of the Kingdom of God, wherefore God's ultimate judgment upon the mighty is also a periodic judgment in history.

III

Let us continue with our bill of particulars. "Not many noble are called." Who are the noble? They are the children and descendants of the mighty. The Greek word which St. Paul uses means the well-born. It is the same words from which "eugenics" is derived. But the connotation of that word is not that of physical or mental health. The well-born are not the healthy. They are the aristocratic. To be well-born means to be born in that circle of society in which to be born is to be well-born. This circular reasoning is an accurate description of the logic by which the children of the mighty arrogate all the virtues of life to themselves because of their favoured position in society.

In every language the words used to designate the favoured few have a double connotation. They designate both social preference and moral worth. The basis of this confusion lies in the identification of manners and morals, a characteristic of every aristocratic estimate of human beings. The Greek word used by Paul (*eugenes*) has exactly the same double connotation as the word noble. To be noble means to be high-minded and to be high-born. "Gentlemen" also has the same double connotation. So has the Latin word *generosus;* also the German *edelig* and *Edelman.* Following the same logic, those who are not aristocratic are bad. The English *villain,* the German *Kerl* and the Latin *malus* all designate the poor who are also the morally evil. Why should they be regarded as lacking moral qualities? Most probably because they have not learned the "gentle" manners of the leisured classes. For to be a gentleman towards a lady means both to deal with her in terms of sincerity and integrity and to bow her into the drawing room with éclat. All these double connotations hide the moral confusion of the mighty in the second and third generation. The first generation of mighty men may be rough fellows who make no claims to gentleness in either manners or morals. But the second generation uses the privileges amassed by the power of the fathers to patronise the arts, to acquire culture, to obscure, consciously or unconsciously, the brutalities of the struggle for power which goes on in every society and which constitutes its very life.

If not many noble are called in the judgment of God, that means that power leads not only to pride and injustice but to hypocrisy. The culture of every society seeks to obscure the brutalities upon which it rests. At its best it is, of course, more than a rational-

isation of the interests of the powerful and a justification of their rule. But at its worst (and this worser
element is never lacking) it hides injustice behind a
façade of beauty. This is why the prophets were so
anti-cultural and condemned the leisured "who in-
vented instruments of music like David" (Amos);
this is why Isaiah was critical of the religious cultus
in which æsthetic qualities became substitutes for
moral honesty: "Bring no more vain oblations; in-
cense is an abomination unto me; the new moons
and sabbaths, the calling of assemblies, I cannot away
with; it is iniquity, even the solemn meeting. . . .
Wash you, make you clean; put away the evil of
your doings from before mine eyes; cease to do evil;
learn to do well; seek judgment, relieve the oppressed; judge the fatherless; plead for the widow."
The opposition of the prophets to the cultus may be
partly prompted by the suggestion of magic in sac-
rificial offerings. But it is significant that the artistic
elaboration of the ritual falls under their condemnation, as well as the burning of sacrifices. "Take thou
away from me," declares Amos in Yahweh's name,
"the noise of thy songs, for I will not hear the melody
of thy violas, but let judgment run down as waters and
righteousness as a mighty stream." These prophetic
judgments are something more than puritan icono-
clasm. They are the expression of mankind's uneasy

conscience about the relationship of culture to social injustice.

The noble are not "called" because they sprinkle rosewater on the cesspools of injustice and because they clothe tyrannical power with broadcloth and surround it with soft amenities, and fool themselves and others by their pretensions. It might be added that not only the second and subsequent generations of the mighty but the women of the mighty men fall particularly under this judgment. Every "lady bountiful" who takes established injustice for granted but seeks to deodorise it with incidental philanthropies and with deeds of kindness, which are meant to display power as much as to express pity; every act of aristocratic condescension by which the traditional reputation of the generosity of the "gentle" has become established, falls under this judgment. The noble are not called in the Kingdom of God, at least not many of them, because they are lacking in inner honesty. But they, as well the mighty, are subjected not only to this ultimate judgment of the Kingdom. They are subjected as well to periodic judgments in history, when what is hidden becomes revealed and society suddenly becomes aware of the moral and social realities, hidden behind the decencies of its political rituals and cultural amenities.

IV

"Not many wise men after the flesh are called." This judgment seems a little more perverse than the others. The wise men will inevitably regard such a judgment as a revelation of the natural obscurantism of the religious prophet. Would not all the problems of society be solved if Plato's dream would only come true and the wise were made the rulers of society? Do not the wise save us from the ignorant caprice of the mighty? And are they not the seers who disclose the hidden secrets of nature and history to us? Why should the wise not be called?

Perhaps, because they are not wise enough. They are not always wise enough to see through the pretensions of the mighty and the noble. Consequently they tend to become servile camp-followers of the mighty. The mighty make history and the wise men after the flesh chronicle their deeds of daring in flattering colours. Just because they have a prestige for impartiality they become the most successful liars. In Julien Benda's *Treason of the Intellectuals* the treason of the "wise men after the flesh" to the truth during the World War is presented in a devastating accumulation of evidence. Even when the wise men are not consciously dishonest, which they are usually not, they are not as wise as they think themselves. They are, at any rate, not wise enough to reach a

perspective which truly transcends the peculiar interests of the group or nations with which they are
intimately associated. Aristotle was not wise enough
to see that his justification of slavery was incompatible
with the facts of human nature and the experience of
history. Plato was not wise enough to see the weaknesses of the Spartan system, which he used as a
model for his utopia. Voltaire was not wise enough
to know that his criticisms of feudalism were inspired
as much by bourgeois perspectives as by the disgust
of a rationalist for superstition. Few of the wise men
of the great nations were wise enough in 1914–18
to do more than clothe the prejudices and express the
passions of their respective nations in more plausible
and credible terms than the ignorant. Much of
what passes for education removes no unwarranted
prejudices but merely gives men better reasons for
holding them.

The wise men stand under a specially severe judgment because every pretense of impartiality makes
partial pronouncements the more inimical to truth.
One of the most instructive facts of human history is
that not the so-called impartial observers of justice
and injustice are clearest in their condemnations of
injustice but rather the poor victims of injustice. Thus
the poor and oppressed must, through the physical
knowledge of the pain they suffer, see some facts and
pronounce some judgments which the wise cannot

see. If God "hath chosen the weak things of the world to confound the things which are mighty; and the base things of the world, and things which are despised," this choice is particularly relevant for the ultimate divine judgment upon life; but it is not without significance for the processes of history.

The wise may not be chosen, not only because they are not wise enough but because they are too wise. Wisdom may overreach itself. Wisdom, like power, tempts men to pride. Sometimes the wise identify truth with rational consistency and seek to measure the paradoxes of life and reality by the canons of human logic. The wise are too wise to see that the world is both "God's world" and (to use a slang phrase) "a hell of a world." Hence the wise tend to be either optimists or pessimists. The mixture of gratitude and contrition which characterises the simple religious heart outrages their sense of consistency. Yet the world is both good and evil and the proper attitude toward it is one of both gratitude for the mercies of God revealed in it and contrition for the evils which human sin has created in it. Whether they are appraising the world or seeking to understand man's place in the cosmos, or estimating the curious mixture of good and evil in the human heart, the wise men usually resolve the paradoxes of religion and arrive at a simpler and more consistent truth which has the misfortune of being untrue to the facts

210

of human existence. The wise either ascribe a significance and dignity to man which denies his creatureliness and finiteness; or they think man insignificant because he is dwarfed by the vastness of the interstellar spaces. They do not understand the truth of the Christian religion which Pascal expressed in the words: "The essence of the Christian religion consists in the mystery of a redeemer who, uniting in himself the two natures, human and divine, has withdrawn men from the corruption of sin to reconcile them to God in His divine person. This teaches us two great truths together, that there is in man a capacity to be like God and at the same time a corruption in his nature which renders him unworthy of God. It is equally important to know both of these truths.—One knowledge produces the pride of the philosopher who knows God but does not know his own misery, the other produces the despair of the atheist who knows his own misery but knows no redeemer."

Most of the great truths of the Christian religion are the foolishness of God which is wiser than the wisdom of men. It is apprehended not by sharpening human wisdom but by humility of spirit.

> "The truth that wise men sought
> Was spoken by a child;
> The alabaster box was brought
> In trembling hands defiled."

211

Sometimes the wise are too wise to act. In their wisdom they see truth and value in every possible alternative of thought and action. So they spend their time balancing one idea against another, unable to achieve any dynamic force. In them the

"native hue of resolution
Is sick'lied o'er by a pale cast of thought."

The wise man may stand on a higher level of life and truth than the mighty man. But he is not free of the temptation to destroy the culture he has created and to destroy it by the same qualities by which he helped to create it. There is, in other words, no type of human eminence which is not subject to the sin of self-destroying pride. Every quality which leads to eminence in human history represents, on one side of it, an extension of a force of nature by which the harmonies of nature are disturbed, the inequalities of nature accentuated, the cruelties of nature aggravated and human history involved in self-destruction. These tragic aspects of human excellence and superiority are usually obscured in history. They become fully apparent only in rare moments when empires and civilisations decay and when it is recognised that they were brought low, not by some external foe but by the defect of their own virtues.

Yet there is in the Christian religion an insight into this matter which does not depend upon the corroboration of history. Even if history did not periodically pass its judgments upon the wise, the mighty and the noble, the words of St. Paul would still be true and would convince those, who view life in terms of the Christian faith, of their truth. The Christian faith is centred in one who was born in a manger and who died upon the cross. This is really the source of the Christian transvaluation of all values. The Christian knows that the cross is the truth. In that standard he sees the ultimate success of what the world calls failure and the failure of what the world calls success. If the Christian should be, himself, a person who has gained success in the world and should have gained it by excellent qualities which the world is bound to honour, he will know nevertheless that these very qualities are particularly hazardous. He will not point a finger of scorn at the mighty, the noble and the wise; but he will look at his own life and detect the corruption of pride to which he has been tempted by his might and eminence and wisdom. If thus he counts all his worldly riches but loss he may be among the few who are chosen. The wise, the mighty and the noble are not necessarily lost because of their eminence. St. Paul merely declares with precise restraint that "not many are called." Perhaps, like the rich, they may enter into the Kingdom of God through the needle's eye.

Eleven:
THE THINGS THAT ARE
AND
THE THINGS THAT
ARE NOT

Yea, and things which are not [*hath God chosen*], *to put to nought things that are.*   *I Corinthians 1:28.*

II: THE THINGS THAT ARE
AND
THE THINGS THAT
ARE NOT

THE CLIMAX of the Pauline transvaluation of values is given in the interesting phrase, "Yea, and things which are not hath God chosen, to put to nought things that are." It deserves special consideration. The previous judgments about the wise and the foolish, the mighty and the weak, the noble and the despised, imply socio-moral conclusions of more revolutionary import than the church had realised. But the observation about the threat of the "things that are not" to "the things that are" raises religious judgments to a plane in which discrimination between wise and foolish, mighty and weak is no longer possible. In the former a philosophy of history is suggested. It is pointed out how in history things which only partially exist (the weak, the foolish and the despised) are used by God against those things which exist fully and therefore imagine themselves to exist necessarily. But in this final

217

climactic word the relation of eternity to history is suggested. The vast possibilities of creation out of "things that are not" are set as a threat against every existing thing.

The relation of this final word to the preceding judgments establishes a perfect norm for the relation of purely religious to religio-moral judgments. Prophetic religion is bound to speak a special word of warning and condemnation to those who are firmly established in history, whether individuals or classes, because they are particularly tempted to imagine themselves the authors and sole protectors of what is good in history. But if this word stands alone a religio-moral insight is easily reduced to a purely political one and religion may thus become a mere tool of the rebellion of the weak against the strong. It must be observed that historic religion has not frequently succumbed to the temptation of this corruption; but its immunity has been due to the fact that it has not frequently understood or pronounced the prophetic word of judgment upon the mighty, wise and noble. Whenever it has learned to speak that word it has also entertained, and frequently succumbed to, the temptation of corrupting it into a purely political judgment.

Against the danger of this temptation stands the further insight that God will take "the things which are not to put to nought things that are." Every life, whether mighty or weak, whether respected or despised in a particular situation, is under the peril of regarding itself as necessary and central in the scheme of things, rather than as contingent and dependent. More accurately, it seeks to overcome the apprehension of its own insignificance by protesting its significance overmuch and implementing this assertion by deeds of imperialism. The weak are no more immune from this temptation than the strong and wise. Whatever the defects of Nietzsche's perverse ethics, he is right in discerning the element of vindictiveness which expresses itself in the rebellion of the weak and the despised. This is not the only element in their rebellion. At best it is, as the rebels assert it to be, a fateful instrument of the judgments of God. Yet no class which resists the sins of the mighty and the noble ever does so with a purely messianic consciousness. Compounded with its purer sense of destiny is a baser metal of wounded ego and compensatory pride and vindictiveness. The disinherited are human, in other words, and therefore subject to basic human sins. The weak will not only sin when they become mighty, but they sin in prospect and imagination while they are weak. The communist denial of this fact is being tragically refuted in contemporary Russian history in which the weak, who have become mighty, are committing all the sins of the mighty of other generations. Siberian exile in

1905 does not guarantee social or moral disinterestedness in the oligarch of today.

The threat of the "things that are not" stands against every life. Every one must therefore decide whether he will accept this threat as a judgment upon his life, or as a challenge to be overcome by increasing the pretension of his life and claiming necessary and independent value for it. This is the decision between religious humility and sinful pride. Perhaps this is something more than a decision; for no one can decide to be humble if the inexhaustible resources of God as enemy and friend have not been revealed to him.

But the question arises whether it is really possible to justify the assertion that God puts to nought the things which are by the things which are not. Ordinarily the things which are not enter into existence by way of some relationship to the things that are. The creative power of God is revealed in them because there is genuine novelty in a new emergence in either nature or history. It is not merely the old thing in a new guise. But on the other hand the creative power of God expresses itself in relation to an already established creation. Whether this created order ought to be regarded as the revelation of the wisdom of God through which his will is proved not to be arbitrary, or whether creation represents a self-

limitation upon God, both will and mind, is a theological problem which we need not explore for our
purposes. It is obvious that nothing appears in either
nature or history which does not bear some relation
to previous things and events. On the other hand,
not every new emergent is an improvement or extension of what has been. Frequently the new destroys
the old. The colossal prehistoric animals must have
seemed in their day to belong indubitably to the
things "that are." They are extinct and only skeletal
remains tell of their once proud and unchallenged
strength.

In the field of history the things "that are" live
in even greater peril than in nature. What has established itself in history is the fruit not only of a natural
development but of a human will. This human will
always extends an impulse of nature beyond the
limits it has in nature. This extension is the basis of
human creativity but also the cause of human sin.
Every human extension of nature therefore contains
the fateful element of an extension of the arbitrary
character of existence in a conscious or unconscious
effort to deny arbitrariness. The mighty make this
effort by increasing their power and seeking to bring
all life under themselves as the unifying principle.
Thus they can give themselves to the illusion that
their life is necessary to the preservation of social

order. They forget on how many different principles and by what varying forces social order has been achieved in human history.

The wise seek the same end by proving that their particular type of existence (and the philosophy which justifies it) represents a final existence and a final philosophy. The reactionary illusions of Hegel, the bourgeois illusions of Comte and the proletarian illusions of Marx are instructive on this point. All of them imagined themselves in possession of both a philosophy and social existence which could not be challenged by the future. They knew very well that the past had been challenged in every moment. But they thought they had arrived at a life and thought which belonged to the "things that are" in an absolute sense. They did not dream of history stopping with their achievements. They merely imagined that it would be bound to them. The future would no longer be a threat but only a promise. This conclusion is the more remarkable in both Hegel and Marx because both of them recognised a dialectic principle (an antithetical threat to existing things) in the history of the past. In other words, the inclination of wise men to imagine that their wisdom has exhausted the infinite possibilities of God's power and wisdom is merely one aspect of the general character of human sin. Human reason is made the servant and slave of human pride. The infinite possibilities in God's hands are foolishly restricted to some little canon of human logic. Usually reason accomplishes this illusory result by the simple expedient of cataloguing the various forms and aspects of existence into various categories and then claiming that because the categories are rational, the contents also are. If it can establish some historical relation between one category and a succeeding one, it imagines that it has fathomed the whole of creativity in some simple law of development. The fact that it regards its own particular category of existence as the last in the whole series of development is partly a natural illusion of the finite mind. But it is partly a conscious or unconscious effort to obscure the irrationality of the future, and to hide the incapacity of the mind to fathom it, and of a contemporary type of existence to bind the future to its own necessities.

Thus every civilisation contemplates the ruin of social orders which preceded it and dreams of its own indestructibility. There is no emancipation from these illusions in any philosophy; for every philosophy is under the illusion that it has no illusions because it has discovered the illusions of its predecessors. There can be emancipation only in the word of God which is spoken to man from beyond all human possibilities. This word must be heard in faith and repentance: in faith, because every effort to comprehend it completely reduces it to some human value; in repentance, because it convicts all life of the sin of pretending to be what it is not.

It is not to be assumed that any nation or social order, any civilisation or culture will ever be convicted by such a word so that it would cease from its pretensions. To the end of history social orders will probably destroy themselves in the effort to prove that they are indestructible. It may not even be assumed that individual man will cease from his pretensions because he has been convicted of them. Yet there is a difference in being a slave to them and being convicted of them. In the latter case the spirit may be free of them, even though man's unconscious actions and attitudes may still be determined by them. In that case men would not escape the tragedy of self-destruction in which all human life is involved; but it would cease to be a tragedy, if fully understood. In that sense the gospel's assurance of redemption is intimately involved in its judgment. Collective man, on the other hand, probably lacks sufficient self-transcendence, ever to hear the word of judgment upon his own pretensions. Wherefore the lives of nations and empires, of cultures and civilisations are involved in recurring tragedy. Each civilisation will imagine that it has overcome the weaknesses and sins which brought death to its predecessors; and it will illustrate the quintessential form of those weaknesses in that very conviction.

This does not mean that cultures and civilisations may not learn various arts and sciences from each other, including the art of social politics. They are thus able to a greater or less degree to ward off the perils of social anarchy and disintegration. Therefore truly wise civilisations have a longer life than foolish ones. The difference in longevity may be a matter of many centuries. In the same way a "good" man preserves his bodily health while the dissolute man dissipates it. What no civilisation or culture has ever done, however, is to admit that the force of a new condition, necessity or power in history, incompatible with its own established presuppositions and privileges, had an equal or superior right to existence with itself. Civilisations meet such a situation with instinctive reactions derived from the impulse of survival. Yet there is always something more than survival impulse in the strategy of cultures and civilisations. That something is derived from human pride. For man cannot fight for his existence without morally justifying himself as the protagonist of values necessary to existence itself. Thus the "things that are" are persuaded into their vain defiance of the "things that are not." The defiance is vain because God is the author of the things that are not. They reveal his creative power as both judgment and mercy upon the things that are.

Twelve:
ZEAL WITHOUT
KNOWLEDGE

Brethren, my heart's desire and prayer to God for Israel is, that they might be saved. For I bear them record that they have a zeal of God, but not according to knowledge. For they being ignorant of God's righteousness, and going about to establish their own righteousness, have not submitted themselves unto the righteousness of God.

For Christ is the end of the law for righteousness to every one that believeth. For Moses describeth the righteousness which is of the law, that the man which doeth those things shall live by them. But the righteousness which is of faith speaketh on this wise, Say not in thine heart, Who shall ascend into heaven? (That is, to bring Christ down from above:) Or, Who shall descend into the deep? (that is, to bring up Christ again from the dead:) But what saith it? The word is nigh thee, even in thy mouth, and in thy heart: that is, the word of faith, which we preach. . . .

For there is no difference between the Jew and the Greek: for the same Lord over all is rich unto all that call upon him. For whosoever shall call upon the name of the Lord shall be saved.

Romans 10:1–13.

12: ZEAL
WITHOUT KNOWLEDGE

THE WORDS, "I bear them witness that they have a zeal of God but not according to knowledge," were spoken by St. Paul with reference to his own people and generation. They nevertheless have a remarkable applicability to the humanistic age which began in the eighteenth century and is now drawing to a close in such a sorry anarchy of international and social wars. Believing itself to be irreligious but wise, it would regard the judgment that it had zeal, but not according to knowledge, with shocked incredulity. Yet the truth is that its confusions arise not from its irreligious knowledge but from its heedless and unwise religion.

The modern age substituted the God of reason and nature for the God of revealed religion. That substitution seemed to be not only "according to knowledge" but according to conscience. The modern man was shocked by traditional religion's defiance of the obvious achievements of modern science; but he was also outraged by the historic affinity between established religion and traditional social injustice.

He championed enlightenment against obscurantism and justice against a pessimistic and deterministic religious acquiescence in injustice. He hoped that if religious prejudices and superstitions could be overcome, reason would establish a common humanity, freed of division and conflict and emancipated of tyranny and oppression. The faith of modernity is most accurately described as a rationalistic humanism. The purpose of the modern rationalist is, by substituting scientific methods and rational disciplines for authoritarian faiths, to unite all men in a common bond of goodwill. Comte, the positivist philosopher of the last century, expressed the faith and hope of modernity in the words: "Unity will be brought about in society, since a new spiritual power, possessed of universally admitted principles, will give all men and women a common education, will teach them all the same morality and will rally them all within the same religion of love and goodness." The identical faith is expressed in John Dewey's recent book *A Common Faith* in which the divisive forces in society are ascribed to anachronistic traditions, chiefly religious, which separate men into warring camps. These divisions will be overcome by a non-authoritarian education which will create a common faith for all men of goodwill.

I

Before seeking to justify the indictment that this faith in the unifying force of human reason is "not according to knowledge" it must be pointed out that history has refuted it more completely than any argument could. The age which began with the dream of a universal brotherhood is ending in a series of fratricidal strifes in which men of different nations and classes are tempted to deny and outrage the last vestige of a common humanity. The significant fact about modern Europe is that the universal aspects of European culture are being completely destroyed. They are consciously denied in the religions of "blood and earth" which place a premium upon national uniqueness. They are as effectively destroyed by the class conflict which rages everywhere in western civilisation and in which fascist and communist refuse to recognise any common ground or similar convictions about the nature of man or history, of life or destiny. Surely a religion of humanity which has failed so completely in realising its intentions and which misjudged the future so hopelessly is under a grave indictment from historical reality, even before any one challenges its characteristic credos.

The charge that this religion is a "zeal of God but not according to knowledge" ought not to be attempted, however, without a grateful appreciation

231

for what was genuinely the zeal of God in it. Modern Christians play the ungrateful fools if they do not do justice to what was really emancipating in the hopes of the modern age. The humanistic age was not entirely wrong, either in what it opposed or in what it affirmed. Humanism opposed the obscurantism to which an authoritarian religion is inevitably tempted when it seeks to transmute the symbols of its faith into adequate descriptions of detailed historical occurrences. A religion which has discovered the limits of human knowledge does not improve the inadequacies of this knowledge if it seeks to shackle culture by religious dogma. Such dogmatism invariably leads to a religious sanctification of the viewpoints of a particular age and the morality of a particular class. Humanism was not to know that its own culture would degenerate into an even more divisive fanaticism, when it first opposed the fanaticism of religion. A genuine passion for humanity animated its opposition to divisive dogmatisms which had leagued God with a particular cultural viewpoint or social position. Though Helvetius was not a profound philosopher, there is nevertheless a wholesome contempt for religious hatred in his *De l'Esprit* which we may still acknowledge gratefully. He said: "On every side you see the consecrated knife of religion raised against the breasts of women and children and the

earth all smoking with the blood of victims, immo-
lated to false gods or the Supreme Being, and present-
ing one sickening, horrible charnel-house of in-
tolerance. . . . What man could fail at such a sight
to be touched with compassion for humanity, and
would not use all his endeavour to found probity,
not on principles so worthy of respect as those of
religion but on principles less easily abused, such as
those of personal interest would be?" In these words
Helvetius spoke for the whole "Enlightenment."

Religious dogmatism not only accentuated in-
tolerance and bigotry but also sanctioned the social
hierarchy of feudal life. It persuaded men that the
fate which made one man master and another slave
was God-ordained. It searched the scripture to justify
slavery and to maintain serfdom. It gave a false
appearance of inexorable destiny to the inequalities
of society, which were frequently no more than the
consequence of natural and historical accidents of
fortune. Thus it enslaved conscience to the caprices
of history. In opposing these tendencies of orthodox
religion the age of reason had the zeal of God. In a
sense the criticisms which it levelled at orthodox
religion were in conformity with the Pauline warning, "Say not in thine heart, Who shall ascend unto
heaven? (that is, to bring Christ down from above)."
Orthodox religion had been tempted to make Christ

a human possession by its church monopoly of salvation and to deny brotherhood to those who do not share this possession.

Modern humanism was as truly religious in some of its affirmations as in some of its criticisms. It affirmed that men possessed a common humanity in their common natural needs. That great spirit of early humanism, Shakespeare, expresses this idea perfectly in the mouth of Shylock: "Hath not a Jew eyes? Hath not a Jew hands, organs, dimensions, senses, affections, passions; fed by the same food, hurt with the same weapons, subject to the same diseases, healed by the same means, warmed and cooled by the same winter and summer, as a Christian is? If you prick us do we not bleed, if you tickle us do we not laugh, if you poison us do we not die and if you wrong us shall we not have revenge?" High cultural elaborations, including religious ones, are always in danger of forgetting this simple fact. It is not only "in Christ," that is ultimately, that men are one; they are one immediately in creation. "God has made of one blood all the nations of men."

Yet the differences which nature, climate, history and destiny cleave into our common animal nature are real. Challenged by these, humanism turned to a more rationalistic faith. Borrowing from the Stoics, it insisted that men were brothers in the common gift of reason. "Hast thou forgotten," said Marcus

234

Aurelius, "how closely all men are allied to one another, not of blood or of seed but of the same mind? Thou hast also forgotten that every man's mind partakes of the deity and no man can properly call anything his own; for all proceeds from that one who is the giver of all life." The Christian will be more circumspect than the stoic Emperor and claim only that all men are created in "the image of God" rather than that they "partake of the deity." Nevertheless, what is asserted here is important. The faith that all men may be "of the same mind" is unfortunately illusory. But it is quite right to assert that they are all the same in having a mind. They are not animals. Having been given a measure of freedom in their reason and imaginations they cannot take their finiteness and temporal limitations for granted as animals do. Their animal nature confronts them with a common fate of mortality and their human nature transmutes this fate, no matter how inexorable, into an occasion for fear, grief and sorrow. Their insertion in nature divides them according to the accidents of geography; their freedom from nature makes their conscience uneasy in these divisions.

A prophetic religion which does not appreciate these affirmations of humanism, as belonging to the prophetic tradition itself, is untrue to its own heritage and false to its duty. Some elements of common decency in human life depend upon a common-sense analysis of the human situation which more profound theologies sometimes obscure. The differences between men are accentuated to-day not only by false religions of "blood and earth" but by false Christian theologies which place an undue religious sanctity upon what they call "the order of creation." These anti-humanistic theologies are false because they ascribe divine intention to the contingencies of nature and history.

II

Nevertheless, we must insist that this humanistic idealism has been a zeal without knowledge. The knowledge it lacked is accurately described in a further word of our text: "For they being ignorant of God's righteousness, and going about to establish their own righteousness, have not submitted themselves unto the righteousness of God." A non-Christian humanism makes human reason God. Reason is the universal value which it sets above all particular values and makes the criterion of all morality. It is by human reason that all history is to be judged. The fatal error of rationalistic humanism is its failure to recognise that reason is universal only in purely formal terms. Logic and mathematics may be universal; but no judgment which fills logical forms with material content is universal. A moral idealism which does not recognise this fact invariably mistakes its particular judgments for genuinely universal judgments, failing to see how it has insinuated its partial and finite perspectives into its supposedly universal standards.

Rationalistic humanism, in other words, forgets the finiteness and creatureliness of man. It does not subject human righteousness to a transcendent righteousness, the righteousness of God. Thus it tempts men to "go about establishing their own righteousness" and finally degenerates into a fanaticism more grievous than that of dogmatic religion. The logic of the decay of modern culture from universalistic humanism to nationalistic anarchy may be expressed as follows: Men seek a universal standard of human good. After painful effort they define it. The painfulness of their effort convinces them that they have discovered a genuinely universal value. To their sorrow, some of their fellow men refuse to accept the standard. Since they know the standard to be universal the recalcitrance of their fellows is a proof, in their minds, of some defect in humanity of the non-conformists. Thus a rationalistic age creates a new fanaticism. The non-conformists are figuratively expelled from the human community.

Sometimes universalistic humanism destroys itself in this fashion. Sometimes it is destroyed by a resurgence of human passions which its too cool and calculating rationalism had outraged. The disciples of

Rousseau have always played a minor role in the drama of modern history, dominated as it was by the disciples of Voltaire and Diderot, of Condorcet and Godwin. But since the former understood and appreciated an element in human nature which the rationalists had left out of account, they are able in these latter days to take vengeance upon their masters. The romantic undercurrent in modern culture has erupted to break and to flood the thin ice of rationalism which had obscured and repressed the vitality of the total human psyche. In their varying emphases, Schopenhauer and Fichte, Nietzsche and Spengler, Freud and Marx have all effectively challenged the rationalist illusion. Yet only one of these critics, Marx, is interested in discovering a basis for a universal culture. The rest are romantics who believe that human vitality is self-justifying, whether expressed in Nietzsche's superman, in Fichte's nation, in Spengler's aristocrat or in Freud's unconscious. Romanticism sets vitality and uniqueness against the universal standards of rationalism. This creed finally degenerates into the belief that might makes right. Hitler and Mussolini are both the offsprings of the romantic movement. Their primitivistic tribalism is the final defeat of rationalistic universalism.

Perhaps we ought not to hold modern rationalism responsible for its defeat at the hands of a more robust romanticism. In history as in nature the fittest do not always survive. Perhaps we ought to regard this capitulation of modern humanism to the superior strength of tribalism as one of those unfortunate fatalities which lends a tragic note to history. This is not the first time that the beasts of the forest have invaded the civilised settlement or that a primitive natural force has blindly crushed some carefully wrought artifact of the human mind. But such a generous judgment does not meet the issue. After all, the fact that romanticism and rationalism are conflicting creeds within the heart of modern culture is proof of the inability of modern man to find a view of human nature which will do justice to all of the facts. If the rationalist imagines that he can tame the vital capacities of natural man simply by a continual extension of education, he is making a serious error which history will disclose and life will avenge. Furthermore, if the romanticist, who begins with as universalistic a dream as the rationalist, turns into a tribalist, this decadence also reveals the error of his romantic view of the problem of man. In the history of modern culture both types of universalism, romantic and rationalistic, have destroyed themselves and each other. The rationalists are unconscious fanatics who still imagine that their ideals of "parliamentary democracy" or of "scientific culture" represent universal human values. The romanticists, on the other hand, are conscious fanatics who have

239

explicitly disavowed their previous universalism. The rationalists mistake the particular viewpoints of a bourgeois civilisation for eternal principles, while the romanticists, with more brutal honesty, point the nationalistic anarchy of late capitalism against its early quasi- and pseudo-universalism. The romantic victory is so easy because the forces of nature are both more powerful in conflict with reason and more implicit in the operations of reason than modernity realised.

There is a peculiar pathos in this final victory of nature (in the form of "blood and earth") over reason, because modern culture had frequently assumed the identity of nature and reason. It spoke of the principles of conduct, which it intended to substitute for the outmoded religious codes, as "laws of nature" or as "laws of reason" indiscriminately. Thus Herder declared: "Upon reason depends the essence of our race, its end and its fate. History teaches to conform to the eternal laws of nature. While it shows us the defects and consequences of all unreason, it teaches us our place in that great organism in which reason and goodness struggle with chaotic forces, always however, according to their nature, creating order and pressing forward to the path of victory." The mistake of identifying reason and nature was inherited by modernity from Stoicism and represents a characteristic error of pantheism. It imagines that the moral ideal for man is given in an established harmony of nature which reason discovers. This is a serious error. Insofar as nature reveals a pre-established harmony it is not moral but amoral. The same freedom of reason which establishes the possibility of moral action also creates confusion and those "chaotic forces" which Herder fondly imagines to have their nemesis in reason.

It is just in the relation of human reason to nature in which the very evil arises, which modern culture hoped to destroy so easily by extending the force of reason. Insofar as human reason really frees the human spirit from the necessities and contingencies of nature it creates the possibilities of moral action. Insofar as this emancipation is never complete and rationality is never discarnate, it accentuates the disharmonies of nature. Thus the same human reason which, on the one hand, regards differences of race as accidents of nature, as contingencies to be discounted and defied in the name of rational brotherhood, also gives these differences a spiritual significance, which they do not have in nature. Race pride and prejudice are just as much the fruits of rational freedom as is inter-racial brotherhood. Likewise the same reason which challenges natural impulses and necessities in the interest of a higher good can raise these very impulses into the semblance of an ultimate good. Sexual impulse can be sublimated and channelled in human behaviour while it is a fixed element in animal life. But sex may also become the perverse centre of human interest and the source of disharmonies, unknown in animal behaviour.

Thus it is obvious that the very reason, which modern culture has regarded as God, as the principle of universality and as the guarantor of goodness, is really man's problem and not his answer to the problem. His effort to establish this reason as God consequently results in fanaticisms, more cruel than those which a false religious orthodoxy had prompted. A human righteousness, which is not subjected to a purer righteousness than anything to be found in nature or history, must inevitably degenerate into a fanatic self-righteousness. The worship of humanity disintegrates into the worship of self. That is the pathos of modern spirituality. This is the consequence of a zeal of God which is not according to knowledge; to the knowledge, namely, of the God who is not the construct of human reason but the presupposition of all thought and life, in short, the creator of the world and its judge.

III

In estimating the errors of modern humanism it would be wrong to include the Marxian humanists too simply into the category of the humanism thus far considered. The Marxian has no illusions about the pretensions of human reason. He knows how closely ideals and interests are related. His whole interpretation of human nature is based upon the recognition of the finiteness of all human culture. Yet by a curious perversity, which can only be regarded as the consequence of natural man's unwillingness to know the God who challenges his good, the Marxian declares that he has found a way of establishing a universal culture, in spite of the finiteness of human thought. He will merely equalise all human interests so that men will not be tempted to prefer their interests to those of others. The *Communist Manifesto* expresses this hope very blandly: "National differences and antagonisms are daily vanishing more and more, owing to freedom of commerce and uniformity in modes of production. The supremacy of the proletariat will cause them to vanish still further. In proportion as antagonism between classes vanishes, the hostility of one nation to another will come to an end. . . . We shall have an association in which the free development of each is the free development of all." The first part of this statement, with its assurance that free commerce and uniform modes of production are causing a daily diminution of national antagonisms, is a striking revelation of the dependence of Marxian thought upon bourgeois rationalistic illusions.

In spite of the higher degree of realism in Marxian thought over general bourgeois culture, its final uni-

243

versalism is as great a delusion as that of the latter. Furthermore history has refuted it just as completely. The violent conflict which has broken out between Stalinites and Trotzkyites can hardly be attributed to the "class conflict." It is a conflict between men equally devoted to a "classless society" and equally informed by its presuppositions. Yet in that conflict there is just as complete a denial of any common humanity as in the struggles of capitalistic society. The Moscow trials have made an effectual end of Marxian universalism. Men who do not know that their conceptions of the good stand under a higher judgment, are as cruel toward their foes who share their general political convictions as toward their "class" foes. They need only to prove that these heretical allies are really class foes, to justify any cruel measure which they may take against them. Perhaps, after all, Trotzky is right in his current accusations against the Soviet régime, right at least in envisaging a "class" struggle between the bureaucrats and the masses. This does not mean that the socialisation of property may not be a genuine gain for social justice. But a "classless" society in the sense that it allows no property distinctions is not a fully classless society; for those who hold authority view problems differently from those who are without authority. Such differences need not lead to fratricidal strife. But they have led to such strife whenever men, viewing life from varying perspectives, refuse to admit that their perspectives colour convictions. Convinced that they have an absolute perspective, they are forced to regard their opponents as traitors to the truth. Thus Marxism, which intended to unify all human perspectives upon the basis of identical economic interests, breeds one of the most cruel conflicts between different types of Marxians. Here, too, we have the zeal of God, but not according to knowledge.

One might sum up this whole tragic self-destruction of humanistic idealism by a word from this same chapter of Romans, which we have chosen as our guide. Modern humanism began by protesting against orthodox Christianity's bringing "Christ down from above"; it ends by seeking to "bring Christ up from the dead." It protests against the church's claim that it has realised the transcendent possibility of life which is incarnated in Christ. It does not believe in transcendence. But it seeks to construct a Christ out of some universal human virtue or capacity. Unfortunately nature and history have relativised everything in human life. This effort therefore has the sorry consequence of accentuating the relativities of history into spiritual pretensions of sinful arrogance.

IV

It is interesting to note that the Pauline gospel has a universalism of its own. "There is no difference," declares St. Paul, "between Jew and Greek: for the same Lord is rich unto all that call upon him." This is the brotherhood of common need rather than of common achievement. Jews and Greeks are alike in this that they are both in need of the mercy of God. To subject human righteousness to the righteousness of God is to realise the imperfection of all our perfections, the taint of interest in all our virtues, and the natural limitations of all our ideals. Men who are thus prompted to humility may differ in their ideals; but they will know themselves one in the fact that they must differ, that their differences are rooted in natural and historic circumstances and that these differences rise to sinful proportions beyond anything which nature knows.

They will not regard either their unities or differences in moral ideals as unimportant. They will know that men are called upon to make fateful decisions in human history and that these decisions sometimes set a son at variance with his father and a daughter with her mother. To subordinate the righteousness to which they are devoted under the righteousness of God does not mean to be less loyal to any cause to which conscience prompts them. Yet they will know that they are finite and sinful men, contending against others who are equally finite and equally sinful. Here the religious perspective crosses the moral perspective in such a way that there is always a possibility that men will be beguiled from devotion to the most genuine moral duties they know. But at its best the sense of Christian humility does not destroy moral ardour. It merely destroys moral arrogance and prevents righteousness from degenerating into self-righteousness. It might have mitigated the fury of a William Lloyd Garrison in his attacks upon slave-owners. Yet it did not destroy John Woolman's passion for the abolition of slavery.

Thirteen:
TWO PARABLES
ABOUT JUDGMENT

When the Son of man shall come in his glory, and all the holy angels with him, then shall he sit upon the throne of glory: And before him shall be gathered all nations: and he shall separate them one from another, as a shepherd divideth his sheep from the goats: And he shall set the sheep on his right hand but the goats on the left. Then shall the King say unto them on his right hand, Come, ye blessed of my Father, inherit the kingdom prepared for you from the foundation of the world: For I was an hungered and ye gave me meat: I was thirsty, and ye gave me drink: I was a stranger, and ye took me in: Naked, and ye clothed me: I was sick, and ye visited me. I was in prison, and ye came unto me. . . .

Then shall he say also unto them on the left hand, Depart from me, ye cursed, into everlasting fire, prepared for the devil and his angels: For I was an hungered, and ye gave me no meat: I was thirsty, and ye gave me no drink: I was a stranger, and ye took me not in: naked, and ye clothed me not: sick, and in prison, and ye visited me not. Then shall they also answer him, saying Lord when saw we thee an hungered, or athirst, or a stranger, or naked, or sick, or in prison, and did not minister unto thee? Then shall he answer them, saying, Verily I say unto you, Inasmuch as ye did it not to one of the least of these, ye did it not to me. And these shall go away into everlasting punishment: but the righteous into life eternal.
Matthew 25:31–46.

For the kingdom of heaven is like unto a man that is an householder, which went out early in the morning to hire labourers into his vineyard. And when he had agreed with the labourers for a penny a day, he sent them into his vine-

yard. And he went out about the third hour, and saw others standing idle in the marketplace, and said unto them; Go ye also into the vineyard, and whatsoever is right I will give you. And they went their way. Again he went out about the sixth and ninth hour, and did likewise. And about the eleventh hour he went out, and found others standing idle, and saith unto them, Why stand ye here all the day idle? They say unto him, Because no man hath hired us. . . . So when even was come, the lord of the vineyard said unto his steward, Call the labourers, and give them their hire, beginning from the last unto the first. And when they came that were hired about the eleventh hour they received every man a penny. But when the first came, they supposed that they should have received more; and they likewise received every man a penny. And when they had received it, they murmured against the goodman of the house, saying, These last have wrought but one hour and thou hast made them equal unto us, which have borne the burden and heat of the day. . . . But he answered one of them and said, Friend, I do thee no wrong: didst thou not agree with me for a penny? . . . Is it not lawful for me to do what I will with mine own? Is thine eye evil, because I am good? So the last shall be first, and the first last.

Matthew 20:1–16.

13: TWO PARABLES
ABOUT JUDGMENT

THE two Parables of the Last Judgment and of the Labourers and the Vineyard emphasise two facets of Christ's teaching which are
usually torn apart to become the bases of conflicting
theologies. The Parable of the Last Judgment por-
trays God as judge who rewards the good and
punishes the evil. The criterion of his judgment, the
principle of ultimate virtue in the sight of God, is
defined as compassionate love toward the needy. The
Parable of the Vineyard pictures God as a generous
master who pays his servants without regard for the
length of their services, *i.e.*, without consideration
for the exact degree of good or evil done in their
lives. This procedure, against which one servant protests in the name of justice, is defended by the master's argument: "Is thine eye evil because I am
good?" The clear implication is that the master is
paying all the servants more than they are worth and
is therefore justified in making no distinction between
the last and the first. It implies the same viewpoint
which Jesus stated more explicitly in the observation

that after we have done all we could we still remain unprofitable servants. In the first parable differences between good and evil in man are declared to be ultimately significant in the sight of God. In the other they are declared to be insignificant.

It would not be quite exact and yet it would not be erroneous to designate the first parable "Pelagian" and the second "Augustinian." Their contrasting emphases lie at the foundation of the moralistic and the supramoralistic notes in the Christian religion. In modern theology the first, more simple and understandable moralistic note has frequently been identified with the Gospels and the second with the Pauline Epistles in an effort to discredit the latter at the expense of the former. The first was supposed to belong to the "simple gospel" of Jesus while the latter was designated as "Pauline" in a judgment which usually presupposed that St. Paul had bedevilled and corrupted the simple gospel by his abstruse theology. For this reason it is helpful to draw the second, supramoralistic note from the Gospels, and more particularly from the parables; though it must be admitted that the logic of the Parable of the Vineyard is explicated in the whole of Pauline literature.

I

The fact is that the contrast between these two parables runs through the whole of biblical thought.

254

It does so necessarily because it does justice to two sides of the ultimate problem of human existence. On the one hand it is true that it makes a difference whether men are good or evil, loving or selfish, honest or dishonest. It makes a real difference, that is, an ultimate difference in the sight of God. On the other hand it makes no difference. No life can justify itself ultimately in the sight of God. The evil and the good, and even the more and the less good are equally in need of the mercy of God.

We find this contrast in the Psalms. In the 1st Psalm we read: "Blessed is the man that walketh not in the counsel of the ungodly, nor standeth in the way of sinners, nor sitteth in the seat of the scornful. But his delight is in the law of the Lord. . . . The ungodly are not so." Here the sheep are separated from the goats. But in the 143d Psalm we have an Augustinian confession: "Enter not into judgment with thy servant: for in thy sight shall no man living be justified."

The prophetic literature abounds in the same contrast. For the sake of brevity let an example from Isaiah suffice. The word of moral judgment and condemnation: "If ye be willing and obedient, ye shall eat the good of the land: but if ye refuse and rebel, ye shall be devoured with the sword . . . cease to do evil; learn to do well; seek judgment, relieve the oppressed, judge the fatherless, plead for the widow," is followed by the promise of mercy: "Come now, let us reason together, saith the Lord: though your sins be as scarlet, they shall be as white as snow; though they be red like crimson, they shall be as wool." The sharp distinction between the good and evil in the word of judgment is transcended in the assurance of forgiveness to the evil in the ultimate promise of mercy.

Even St. Paul, who sums up the main emphasis of his gospel in the words, "For there is no difference: for all have sinned, and come short of the glory of God; being justified freely by his grace," is not lacking in the note of moral distinction. He declares: "We must all appear before the judgment seat of Christ; that every one may receive the things done in his body, according to that he hath done, whether it be good or bad."

Nor it is necessary to confine the contrast in the thought of Jesus to the two mentioned parables. The Parable of the Pharisee and Publican is perhaps the most classical expression of Jesus' preference for the contrite sinner to the righteous man who does not know that he is not righteous. Yet his insistence upon the difference between righteousness and unrighteousness can be expressed in words of terrible earnestness "Woe unto the world because of its offences! for it must needs be that offences come; but woe to that man by whom the offence cometh. . . . It were better for him that a millstone were hanged about his neck."

The difference between good and evil in history is an ultimate difference which transcends the relativities of history. The love shown to "one of the least of these my brethren" is love to God Himself. That is, the "good" deed, which in the gospel is always a loving deed, is one which enters into the very texture of eternal reality. Yet on the other hand eternal reality is determined by God and not by man. And it is revealed in the divine mercy which overcomes the evil in man and therefore the distinction between good and evil in man. It makes a difference. It makes no difference. This is the sharp contrast in biblical thought. Let us analyse both parts of this contrast more fully in terms of human experience before we consider a possible ultimate resolution of the contrast.

II

It makes a difference whether men are good or evil and whether they do good or evil. In spite of all moral relativism we know fairly well what good and evil are. Utilitarian moral schemes may justify egotism to a larger degree than the gospel ethic. But there is no system of morals which does not in some way or other give moral preference to the other-regarding rather than the self-regarding act. We know that it is good to restrain the sinful tendency of the self, to live its life at the expense of other life and to strengthen the impulses by which it is bound to other life. Love is the law of life and not merely some transcendent ideal of perfection. All men may violate the law of life but there is a difference between those who seek to draw all life into themselves, and those who have found in God the centre of existence and through loyalty to Him have learned to relate themselves in terms of mutual service to their fellows. There was a difference between John Woolman, the Quaker saint, who felt the sorrows of the slaves as his own, and some pious slave-owner who used the Scripture to justify slavery and to obscure the indecency of one man owning another man as property. There was a difference between the megalomaniac Nero, delighting in cruelty and the gentle Marcus Aurelius, ruling over the same Empire but brooding with pity upon the evils of the world. There is a difference (to go from the imperial throne to the monastic life for examples) between the asceticism of a St. Jerome with his morbid preoccupation with self and that of the joyous, gentle and ecstatic St. Francis. The difference between such men continues to affect the very texture of life in centuries after their existence.

Truth is a virtue and the lie is evil. There is a difference between men of integrity and deceivers. There is a difference between the honest scholar who devotes infinite patience to the task of separating the wheat from the chaff in the records of an age and the tendencious propagandist who makes history lie in favour of his cause. My lie strikes my fellowman with blindness. It prevents him from seeing truly what he might have seen through my eyes. Dishonesty destroys lives. There is a difference between the *Manchester Guardian* and the Rothermere press. Lying has been developed into a high art by the modern political propagandist. If the devil is a liar Doctor Goebbels may find a place of great eminence in the devil's domain. We will never create even the most tentative world community if those who have become our eyes and ears in a technical civilisation will not be more honest with us than they now are, and tell us truly what they see and hear.

Courage is a virtue and cowardice is evil. There is a difference between the brave men who are fighting in Germany through these years for the freedom of the Christian gospel and time-serving ecclesiasts who cravenly submit to the pretentious claims of ridiculous Cæsars, while justifying their capitulation with quotations from Scripture (usually Romans 13). The courage of Thomas More in defying Henry VIII has the quality of eternity in it. It still affects the life of the church, helping weak men to be strong.

There is a difference between peacemakers and warmakers; between those who seek, as much as in

259

them lieth, to live peaceably with all men, and those who wreck the peace and order of communities and nations irresponsibly and recklessly. There is a significant special blessing for the peacemakers in the Beatitudes.

We know that selfish and unselfish people make a difference in our own happiness. Men differ at times in defining virtue and vice. Yet, on the whole, we are fairly clear about the difference between what destroys and what preserves life, what stultifies and what develops human character. These differences are immediately apparent in our experience. But we also sense something of their ultimate significance. We feel that the good and evil of the moment echo through eternity; that each produces a whole series of similar qualities in its train. Omar Khayyam is right:

"The Moving Finger writes; and, having writ,
  Moves on: nor all your Piety nor Wit
  Shall lure it back to cancel half a Line,
  Nor all your Tears wash out a Word of it."

The ultimate judgment of Christ is not merely ultimate in time. The time symbol, that is the "last" judgment, is simply the only way in which this ultimate character in terms of quality can be stated. Each moral act stands under an ultimate judgment in every moment of time. What we do to one of the least of these our brothers is done unto Christ.

Genuine virtue is an act in obedience to God's will and thereby participates in God's creative purpose. An evil act on the other hand is destructive. And in one sense at least destruction has eternal significance. What we destroy we cannot re-create. The life which is destroyed by our heedlessness or greed or lust for power or our sensual passion may be restored by the grace of God; but from our perspective the evil we have done is eternal. Acts of restitution may mitigate the evil but they cannot completely efface its consequences. This emphasis upon the inexorable character of divine judgment is validated in every page of history and in every human experience.

III

Yet there is this other side of the gospel teaching and of all biblical thought: It makes no difference whether men are good or evil in the sight of God, because they are all in need of God's mercy. It makes no difference whether they have laboured long or briefly in the vineyard, the first is as much in need of divine grace as the last. It is because the first are so greatly tempted to forget this that they frequently become last and the last first. It must be admitted that it is difficult to retain and appreciate this "Augustinian" emphasis in the Christian religion, without running the danger of depreciating genuine moral distinctions and of encouraging indifference toward moral striving. This danger is so great that the emphasis would not be justified if it did not justify itself in the actual experience of man. But any careful analysis of human sinfulness proves how important this insight is.

Such an analysis leads first of all to the conclusion that every high type of righteousness is accompanied by its own characteristic sin. We may appreciate the difference between the selfish and the unselfish man but we ought to know that the man who achieves a reputation for virtue and generosity will be assailed by temptation to spiritual pride and vanity, to which he will partly succumb. If he should try consciously to overcome this temptation he may even express pride in his very protestations of humility. "Discourses on humility," said Pascal, "are sources of pride to the vain. Few men speak humbly of humility." Nothing could be more disconcerting to human self-esteem than the discovery in a survey of modern theological thought to what degree theologies which emphasise contrition and humility may become vehicles of the intellectual arrogance of their proponents. The self, wrote the Anglo-Catholic mystic Mrs. Hermann some years ago, is like an onion. Skin upon skin of self must be peeled off, if egotism is to be overcome. The simile is particularly instructive. It reveals the self-defeating character of mystical efforts to eliminate the egoistic element in

262

thought by conscious attacks upon the self; for the onion becomes increasingly pungent as more and more skins are peeled off and is reduced to nothing when the process is completed. The increased pungency symbolises the preoccupation with self involved in the mystical effort to eliminate self; and its final destruction in the process might well stand for the ideal of self-annihilation and absorption in God which is the goal of mysticism. The relation of ego and egotism is really more difficult than is assumed in such an attack upon it.

Every legitimate expression of the ego involves an illegitimate accentuation of its interests, which may take more and more subtle forms, but which can neither be eliminated in historic existence nor yet regarded as normative or good. A recognition of this fact involves the rejection of the Catholic conception of sainthood. Men may be saints, comparatively speaking. They may achieve remarkable heights of imaginative virtue, compared with the grosser and more common forms of self-expression. But they would cease to be saints at the moment in which they regarded themselves as such. Their appreciation by others as saints need not have the same destructive consequence, particularly not if the estimate were made by subsequent generations. But such estimates are still less than accurate if they fail to appreciate the positive evil which every form of virtue distills in human existence. Saints are still sinners, not merely because they fall short of some ultimate norm in their finiteness; but because they are bound to reveal some sinful blindness to their very finiteness, some sinful pretension exceeding their virtue in their very achievements.

"Let us not have a theology," said a theologian recently, "which will equate Hitler and Calvin and insist that both are sinners in equal degree before God." The demand is correct insofar as it insists upon the difference between conscious self-glorification in defiance of God and unconscious egotism which may express itself in the very act of worshipping God. But the very choice of this illustration proves the error in too moralistic estimates of human nature. What the discerning eye of divine wisdom may ultimately determine about the relative virtues of Cæsars and prophets of religion is not given to our minds to anticipate. But we do have enough discernment to realise that on certain levels of moral judgment, which even we can achieve, Hitler and Calvin are strikingly similar. Calvin's dishonesties and brutalities in dealing with Servetus and Castellio are significant examples of the positive evils of sinful pride and even of subtle sadism into which those who are zealous for the Lord may fall. That would be equally true if we compared any two wielders of political power and preachers of divine judgment.

264

Not only is there an element of positive evil in even the most virtuous life. We are also equally sinners in the sight of God because we all fall short in terms of our sins of omission. There is no possibility of arriving at a state of perfection where one could dispense with the confession that we have "left undone the things we ought to have done." We may do no murder; but men perish because we are heedless of their welfare. We may not commit adultery and yet not escape the infraction of the seventh commandment if we think of the commandment in terms of the extension of its meaning in the Sermon on the Mount. We may not bear false witness against our neighbour by conscious word. Yet all men are liars if the unconscious processes by which they betray themselves are considered.

It is one of the curious ironies of modern culture that in the very moment in which a rationalistic type of Christianity tended to consider the possibilities of human perfection in terms of its purely conscious activity, a secular science in the form of psychology on the one hand, and of social economics on the other, revealed the labyrinthian depths of the unconscious and the endless possibilities of evil which were hidden there. Both Marx and Freud have, each in his own way, discovered the unconscious dishonesties which dog human actions and corrupt human ideals, even though the conscious mind is intent upon virtue. The unconscious sins, of which all men are guilty, are sometimes interpreted in purely negative terms. They are supposed to represent the inertia of nature operating against the moral ambitions of the spirit. Yet there are, strictly speaking, no purely negative sins. The natural impulse, which is subtly compounded with devotion to ideals in human behaviour, is never purely natural; that is, it is not merely the animal in man, contending against the distinctively human. The freedom of the human spirit reaches down into the furthest depths of nature and disturbs its natural tranquillity, endowing natural passions with a potency unknown in the animal world. The fantastic images of our dream world, in which passions outlawed by conscience dance their defiance of our conscious laws, are the fruits of the spirit and not of nature. When the animal in us wars against the spirit, it uses weapons stolen from the arsenal of the spirit.

The positive sins of the spirit are Promethean. The spirit of man proudly o'erleaps its moral infirmities and claims an unlawful divinity. The negative sins of man are Dionysian. In them the spirit sharpens all the dark unconscious impulses of nature and sets them at war with the requirements of virtue. Therefore what seems to be negative is not purely negative. When we leave undone the things we ought to have done we are busy doing those things which

we ought not to have done. We are prevented from
virtue by slavery to passions which exert a more cruel
mastery than the inertia of nature. The cruelty of
peasant life in Russia, as depicted by both Tolstoi
and Maxim Gorki, is not merely the consequence of
peasant sloth and ignorance.

There is consequently no solution for the problem
of life on the purely moral level. If there is no
assurance of a divine mercy which not only creates
but re-creates in the wake of human destruction, the
human enterprise remains purely tragic. This is the
justification for the supramoral not in all profound
Christian thought, offensive as this note may be to
all simple moralists who never measure the heights
and depths of life but arrange their neat systems of
morality on the superficial surface of conscious
behaviour.

IV

It is not easy to harmonise the two elements in
the Christian religion which do justice to the two
facets of human experience, the moral and the supramoral. The Pauline doctrine of justification by faith
declares that those who live by faith are declared
righteous by the grace of God even though they are
not righteous by their own achievements. This justification does not absolve man of his moral obligations. God forbid, that we "should sin in order that

grace may abound." On the contrary, the grace of forgiveness is vouchsafed only to those who have consciously made the will of God their law of life. In this sense the tension between law and grace is resolved in the life of the individual.

We can hardly claim, however, that the mystery of their relation to each other is finally cleared for us. The mystery is that on the one hand duty is demanded of us as if duty not done will never be done. On the other hand faith declares that man would be undone if God could not complete what we have left incomplete and purify what we have corrupted. The cross is the perfect revelation of both of these truths. In it the sin against man is revealed as the sin against God, as something more than a casual imperfection. Yet in it the merciful purpose of God, to take human evil into himself and smother it there, is also declared. But even in the cross the relation of law and mercy remains a mystery. We do not know in what sense the evil which we do has eternal significance if we also believe that God overcomes evil. Here Christian truth transcends human wisdom and speaks to us as the foolishness of God which is wiser than the wisdom of men. Yet we are able to accept this foolishness as wisdom if we have probed deeply enough into life to discredit the little systems of wisdom which have pretended to exhaust its mysteries.

Love is both the fulfilment and the negation of

law. Forgiveness is the highest justice and the end of justice. The judge of the Parable of the Last Judgment is inexorable. He consigns men to hell for the evil they have done. The householder of the Parable of the Vineyard specifically rejects the calculations of justice. This judge and this householder are both symbols of God, of the God who is at once judge and redeemer.

Fourteen:
THE KINGDOM
NOT OF THIS WORLD

Pilate therefore entered again into the judgment hall and called Jesus, and said unto him, Art thou the king of the Jews? Jesus answered him, Sayest thou this of thyself, or did others tell it thee of me? Pilate answered, Am I a Jew? Thine own nation and the chief priests delivered thee unto me: what hast thou done?

Jesus answered, My kingdom is not of this world: if my kingdom were of this world, then would my servants fight, that I should not be delivered to the Jews: but now is my kingdom not from hence. Pilate therefore said unto him, Art thou a king then? Jesus answered, Thou sayest that I am a king. To this end was I born and for this cause came I into the world, that I should bear witness unto the truth. Every one that is of the truth heareth my voice. Pilate saith unto him, What is truth?

John 18:33.

14:   THE KINGDOM
NOT OF THIS WOLRD

THE Fourth Evangelist is not an historian but an interpreter of history. His record of the scene of Jesus before Pilate may therefore not be literal history. It is nevertheless a profoundly true drama. It is, in fact, an ageless drama, to which belong as individual acts the records of prophets standing before kings, and appealing to a higher judgment than that by which the king judges them. Jesus before Pilate is the climax of this drama. Here the incarnation of the Judge of the world is judged by the world —and judges it.

We may imagine Pilate the typical wielder of political power. Toward Jesus he had that attitude of mingled admiration and contempt which the man of power usually displays toward the power of pure goodness. It represents a majesty beyond his comprehension and yet a weakness in the domain in which he is master. Pilate's chief interest in Jesus was to determine whether his type of kingship represented a real threat to the Roman imperium. The chief priests had insisted that it did. In their indictments of Jesus before the Jewish court they had emphasised the religious implications of the Messianic idea and had accused him of blasphemy. Before the Roman court they emphasised the political implications of the Messianic idea (which Jesus had, incidentally, specifically disavowed) and accused him of treason. What Pilate wanted to know was whether this man before him was really a harmless religious dreamer and prophet or a dangerous insurrectionist. It may be observed in passing that the judgments of worldly courts are always weighted by that consideration. The most dangerous criminal is always the person who threatens the system which maintains the court itself. No court is ever impartial when questions of its own existence are involved, not even when, as in modern government, the judicial function is separated from executive power. This was the significance of his question: "Art thou the king of the Jews?"

I

Jesus' answer must have quieted Pilate's fears immediately: "My Kingdom is not of this world." With that assurance Pilate relaxed. All the Pilates and Cæsars of the world have been relieved by similar assurances. The Kingdom of God, the kingdom of truth, is not of this world. Therefore the kingdoms of the world need not fear it. Its servants do not fight. They do not set power against power. The kingdoms of the world fear only power. Religion is, after all, a very innocuous vagary. It prompts men to dream of another world in which the injustices of this world will be righted and the sorrows of this world will be turned into joy. Why should not such dreams and such hopes persuade men to suffer present pains with patience? That question has suggested itself to every man of power through the ages. By it he is tempted to offer the prophet and priest of religion a position of auxiliary ruler in his kingdom. We know from history how frequently the offer is accepted.

Even when the prophet or priest is not consciously drawn into partnership with the ruler, the kingdom of which he is the messenger may support the kingdoms of the world. The sanctuary which the priest builds may be a thing of beauty to which men periodically escape from an ugly world, securing just enough relief from oppression to be beguiled from their rebellion against evil. The kingdom of righteousness of which the prophet speaks tempts men to feed on hopes when they are starved by realities. How could the Negroes of the days of slavery have borne their oppression, if they had not been able to sing:

"When I go to heaven, I'll put on my shoes
And I'll walk all over God's heaven"?

Oswald Spengler, the most brilliant apostle of

political reaction in the modern day, has lifted this possible use of religion into a perfect system. A good priest, in his view, is one who persuades men that their hopes and dreams of perfection are not for this world. A bad priest is one who transmutes religious hopes into political discontent. Communism and every other political protest against injustice is thus, in his view, the illegitimate offspring of Christian perfectionism. Let Pilate be assured. Let the fears of Cæsar be dispelled. The Lord has said "My Kingdom is not of this world." Furthermore he has instructed his disciples to "Render unto Cæsar the things that are Cæsar's." Upon that assurance Pilate is able to report, "I find no fault in him"; and all who believe that religion is relevant to the world must be a little embarrassed by Pilate's acquittal. If Jesus' Kingdom does not threaten Pilate's kingdom any more than Pilate assumes, how can it overcome the injustice of Pilate's kingdom? How can it speak a word of legitimate hope to the victims of oppressive power?

II

Before we accept Pilate's complacency as justified it would be well to inquire further into the nature of this kingdom which is not of this world. Jesus defined it as a kingdom of truth: "To this end was I born, and for this cause came I into the world that I should bear witness unto the truth." The Johannine Gospel, speaking particularly to the Greek world, makes much of the idea of truth and of light as the meaning of the Incarnation. It does not, however, regard the truth as some simple proposition which the natural reason of man can grasp. The truth is rather a revelation of the fundamental pattern of life which sin has obscured and which Christ restores. The Logos is the very pattern of the world. "All things were made by him; and without him was not any thing made that was made." The world is in darkness of sin and does not comprehend this light. The pattern of life comes unto his own but his own receive him not. Yet as many as receive him may become sons of God.

The world is, in other words, alienated from its true character. Men do not know their true relation to God. Therefore they make themselves God and their minds are darkened by the confusion caused by this self-glorification. The kingdom of truth is consequently not the kingdom of some other world. It is the picture of what this world ought to be. This kingdom is thus not of this world, inasfar as the world is constantly denying the fundamental laws of human existence. Yet it is of this world. It is not some realm of eternal perfection which has nothing to do with historical existence. It constantly impinges upon man's every decision and is involved in every action.

It is important to recognise that the Kingdom of

God, according to the biblical conception, is never purely an other-worldly perfection, not even when it is interpreted in a gospel which is directed primarily to the Greek world. The Christian is taught to pray constantly "Thy Kingdom come." The hope of this prayer, when vital, is a constant pressure upon the conscience of man in every action.

The kingdom which is not of this world is thus in this world, through man and in man, who is in this world and yet not altogether of this world. Man is not of this world in the sense that he can never rest complacently in the sinful standards which are normative in the world. He may be selfish but he cannot accept selfishness as the standard of conduct. He may be greedy but he knows that greed is wrong. Even when his actions do not conform to his ideals he cannot dismiss his ideals as irrelevant. Modern as well as ancient theologies which emphasise the total depravity of man fail to do justice to the difference between human ideals and human actions. The action may always be sinful but it stands under the criticism of the ideal. Every ideal of justice may be coloured by interest when it is applied to situations in which men are themselves involved; but they cannot consciously construct ideals of justice to conform to their interests. Every corruption of justice can exist only by borrowing from, and pretending to be, a more disinterested justice than it is. This vision of perfection is really what is intended in the stoic conception of the golden age and the Christian idea of perfection before the Fall. To relegate it to an historical period before an historical Fall is to take religious myths too literally and become confused by their historical symbols.

The kingdom which is not of this world is always in this world in man's uneasy conscience. Even in Plato, who is more inclined than biblical thought to relegate perfection to another world, the kingdom which is not of this world is never wholly irrelevant to human actions. At the close of the fourth book of his *Republic* Plato describes the perfect justice to which the wise man will devote himself, and discusses its relation to historical actualities in a dialogue between Socrates and Glaucon:

"To this nobler purpose the man of understanding will devote the energies of his life. He will not allow himself to be dazzled by the foolish applause of this world and heap up riches to his own harm. He will look to the city that is within him and see that no disorder occur there. . . ."

"Then if that is his motive," said Glaucon, "he will not be a statesman. By the dog of Egypt he will. In the city which is his own he certainly will, though in the land of his birth perhaps not.

"I understand," said Glaucon, "you mean that he will be a statesman in the city of which we are the founders and which exists in idea only, for I do not believe that there is such a one anywhere on earth."

"In heaven," I replied, "there is laid up a pattern of it methinks which he who so desires may behold and, beholding, may set his house in order. But whether such a one exists or ever will exist is no matter. For he will live after the manner of that city and have nothing to do with any other."

One is reminded, by this dialogue, of Jesus' words to his disciples when they joyfully reported that "even the devils are subject unto us through thy name." He answered: "Rejoice not, that the devils are subject unto you; but rather rejoice, because your names are written in heaven." There is, in other words, a particular power in the kingdom not of this world over this world, precisely because it does not ask to have its standards validated by worldly success. Its servants may not fight Pilate but they are able to defy Pilate with a cool courage which is not derived from this world.

There is this difference, however, between Plato's and the gospel's conception of the relation of the kingdom not of this world to the world: Plato's is a very individualistic conception. "Whether such a one exists *or ever will exist* is no matter," he declares. He is content to let the individual conscience defy the world without reference to the possible triumph of righteousness in the world. The biblical conception of the Kingdom of God is of an ultimate triumph in, or at least at the end of, history. For the Greek, perfection remains in heaven, because history is by its very character of temporality a corruption of it. In the biblical conception the sin of the world is not due to its temporal character but to man's rebellion against God. Christianity is therefore less confident than Plato that the wise man will obey the vision of perfection which intrigues him; but it is more confident that God will be able to overrule the sinfulness of man.

III

Even though we recognise the relevance of the Kingdom of God to every thought and action in the world, we have not yet faced the significance of Pilate's contemptuous sneer, "What is truth?" What indeed is truth or justice, no matter how high our conceptions may be in the abstract, when each man and nation is able to interpret and to corrupt the truth for its and for his purposes? That sneer comes significantly from a man of power and has particular significance in our own day. For we are living in a day in which new national religions are explicitly disavowing the universal validity of truth. Each nation fashions truth unashamedly in its own interest. Modern fascism thus explicitly affirms the relativity of truth which is implicitly involved in all human actions. If we mean by "the world" only the realm of actuality, the Kingdom of God is quite obviously not in it. It may be in the conscience of man but not in his action. The same man who dreams of an ideal justice or a perfect love acts according to his own interests when he ceases to contemplate and engages in action.

"No deed is all its thought had been,
No will but feels the fleshly screen,"

in the words of Robert Browning.

It is this fact which persuades certain types of Continental theology to regard the Kingdom of God as revealed in the Gospels as only a principle of judgment upon the world and not as a criterion of judgment in the world. In their view the world continues to live by purely egotistic standards and in the inevitable conflict of interests which results from such behaviour. Even the Christian must submit to these standards. If he succeeds in forgiving an enemy or loving a neighbour he must not expect such actions to change the quality of the world's life. Actions inspired by the truth of the Kingdom of God are merely symbols of judgment and hope set in a world which is destroying itself by its sin.

Perverse as such conceptions are, they have, at least, the merit of calling attention to the fact that the sinful world is not as easily transmuted into the Kingdom of God as modern theology had supposed. In one sense the Kingdom of God remains outside the world. The same Pilate who found no fault in Jesus became nevertheless his executioner. The power of Rome felt itself for the moment secure against the threat of this kingdom. But the power of the priests was not secure and they therefore insisted on his destruction. The fact that Pilate, the symbol of power, became the unwilling tool of the priests, is an instructive bit of history. The ambitions of the powerful are never quite as inimical to the Kingdom as the confusion of priests and prophets who are less cynical and more fanatical than Pilate, having mixed truth with sin in a more confusing mixture. Whether it is the state or the church through which we act, the Lord is crucified afresh in every human action.

Nevertheless the kingdom of truth constantly enters the world. And its entrance descends beyond conscience into action. The word is made flesh. The spiritual descendants of Pilate in Germany today are facing a determined band of spiritual sons of the Christ, and the former have found no way of quieting the defiance of the latter by their use of power. No threats of coercion and imprisonment have been able to change the actions of men whose primary loyalty is to God and not to some prince of the world. Their slogan, "We must obey God rather than man," has became a word of nemesis for those who sought to make power the sole source of truth.

The fact that it is the church in modern Germany which defies the state, while many apostles of a universal culture and a universal science have capitulated, is most instructive in regard to the relation of the kingdom not of this world to this world. The university was the pride of Germany; and the German church was more or less moribund. Yet the former has allowed its universal culture to be corrupted by the state while the latter has fought valiantly against such corruption. The culture of the university sought universal truth through the genius of the wise man; and forgot that the wise man is also a sinner, whose interest, passion and cowardice may corrupt the truth. The kingdom of truth which rests upon human wisdom is obviously of this world; so much so that the world may conquer it and reduce its pride to humiliation.

The only kingdom which can defy and conquer the world is one which is not of this world. This conquest is not only an ultimate possibility but a constant and immediate one. In every moment of existence those "who are of the truth" hear the Christ's voice, warning, admonishing and guiding them in their actions. The real truth condemns their lies; pure justice indicts their injustice; the law of love reveals their selfishness; and the vision of God reveals their true centre and source of existence. They may continue to be disobedient to the heavenly vision; but they can never be as they have been.

The kingdom which is not of this world is thus a

more dangerous peril to the kingdoms of the world than any competing worldly kingdom. One nation may be destroyed by another more powerful nation. But civilisations and cultures in their larger historical development are never destroyed by external enemies without first having destroyed themselves. The force of their destruction is not only their own violation of the law of life but the loss of their moral authority under the challenge of those who speak against their power in the name of the Kingdom of God. Pure power cannot maintain itself. It must have some measure of moral respect. It must be admitted that pure conscience seldom defeats an unjust social system. Those who speak against its injustice are primarily its victims. Yet slavery would have persisted if only the slaves had recognised its oppression. A moral element thus enters into every successful challenge of Cæsar's authority.

It is hardly necessary to draw the conclusion from this fact that those who draw their inspiration from Christ's Kingdom must limit themselves to purely moral weapons in contending against historic injustice. Conscience may prompt the challenge of power by power, though it must recognise that the new justice, which emerges from the resulting conflict, will be less than the perfect justice in the name of which it initiated the conflict. The Kingdom of God is relevant to every moment of history as an ideal possibility

285

and as a principle of judgment upon present realities. Sometimes it must be obeyed in defiance of the world, though such obedience means crucifixion and martyrdom. Sometimes courageous obedience forces the evil of the world to yield, thus making a new and higher justice in history possible. Sometimes the law of the Kingdom must be mixed with the forces of nature which operate in the world, to effect at least a partial mitigation of oppression. Martyrs, prophets and statesmen may each in his own way be servants of the Kingdom. Without the martyr we might live under the illusion that the kingdom of Cæsar is the Kingdom of Christ in embryo and forget that there is a fundamental contradiction between the two kingdoms. Without the successful prophet, whose moral indictments effect actual changes in the world, we might forget that each moment of human history faces actual and realisable higher possibilities. Without the statesman, who uses power to correct the injustices of power, we might allow the vision of the Kingdom of Christ to become a luxury of those who can afford to acquiesce in present injustice because they do not suffer from it.

Fifteen:
THE FULFILMENT
OF LIFE

I believe in the forgiveness of sins, the resurrection of the body and the life everlasting.   The Apostles' Creed.

15: THE FULFILMENT
OF LIFE

THESE closing words of the Apostolic creed, in which the Christian hope of the fulfilment of life is expressed, were, as I remember it, an offense and a stumbling-block to young theologians at the time when my generation graduated from theological seminaries. Those of us who were expected to express our Christian faith in terms of the Apostolic creed at the occasion of our ordination had long and searching discussions on the problem presented by the creed, particularly by this last phrase. We were not certain that we could honestly express our faith in such a formula. If we were finally prevailed upon to do so, it was usually with a patronising air toward the Christian past, with which we desired to express a sense of unity even if the price was the suppression of our moral and theological scruples over its inadequate rendering of the Christian faith.

The twenty years which divide that time from this have brought great changes in theological thought, though I am not certain that many of my contemporaries are not still of the same mind in which they were then. Yet some of us have been persuaded to take the stone which we then rejected and make it the head of the corner. In other words, there is no part of the Apostolic creed which, in our present opinion, expresses the whole genius of the Christian faith more neatly than just this despised phrase: "I believe in the resurrection of the body."

The idea of the resurrection of the body can of course not be literally true. But neither is any other idea of fulfilment literally true. All of them use symbols of our present existence to express conceptions of a completion of life which transcends our present existence. The prejudice that the conception of the immortality of the soul is more believable than that of the resurrection of the body is merely an inheritance from Greek thought in the life of the church. One might perhaps go so far as to define it as one of the corruptions which Hellenistic thought introduced into biblical, that is, Hebraic thinking. It is, of course, not absent from the Bible itself. Hellenic and Hebraic conceptions of the after-life wrestled with each other in the mind and the soul of St. Paul; and his dictum, "Flesh and blood cannot inherit the Kingdom of God," belongs to the Greek side of the debate. Whatever may be the truth about the degree of Greek thought in either the Pauline Epistles or the Johannine literature, there can be no question that the dominant idea of the Bible in regard to the ultimate fulfilment of life is expressed in the conception of the resurrection. This is also true of the entire history of the Christian Church until, at a recent date, it was thought that the conception of immortality was more in accord with reason than the idea of resurrection.

This latter prejudice is easily refuted. It is no more conceivable that the soul should exist without the body than that a mortal body should be made immortal. Neither notion is conceivable because reason can deal only with the stuff of experience; and we have no experience of either a discarnate soul or an immortal body. But we do have an experience of a human existence which is involved in the processes of nature and yet transcends them. It is conscious of them and possesses sufficient freedom from them to analyse, judge, modify and (at times) defy them. This human situation is a paradoxical one and it is therefore not easy to do justice to it without falling into the errors of either naturalism or dualism.

I

The idea of the resurrection of the body is a profound expression of an essential element in the Christian world-view, first of all because it expresses and implies the unity of the body and the soul. Through all the ages Christianity has been forced to combat, and has at times capitulated to, the notion, that the significance of history lies in the banishment of the good soul in an evil body and in the gradual emancipation of the soul from the body. Involved in this conception, which is expressed most consistently in Neo-platonism, is the idea that finiteness and particularisation are of themselves evil and that only the eternal is good. Pure spirit is thus conceived as an eternal principle, which is corrupted by its very individualisation in time. Salvation is consequently thought of as release from physical life and temporal existence. In these latter days such conceptions have been related to modern individualism and made to yield the idea of personal survival. But in its more classical and consistent forms this dualism involved the destruction of individuality, so that salvation meant the release from all particularisation and individualisation and reabsorption into the oneness of God.

In contrast to such forms of dualism it must be recorded that the facts of human experience point to the organic unity of soul and body, and do not substantiate the conclusion, suggested by a superficial analysis, that the evil in human life arises from the impulses of the flesh.

Soul and body are one. Man is in nature. He is, for that reason, not of nature. It is important to emphasise both points. Man is the creature of necessity and the child of freedom. His life is determined by natural contingencies; yet his character develops by rising above nature's necessities and accidents. With reference to the purposes of his life, it is significant that the necessities of nature are accidents and contingencies. Sometimes he is able to bend nature's necessities to his own will; sometimes he must submit his destiny to them. But whether he dominates or submits to nature, he is never merely an element in nature. The simple proof is that his life is not wholly determined but is partly self-determining. This is a very obvious fact of experience which is easily obscured by philosophies, which either lift man wholly out of nature or make him completely identical with it, usually for no better reason than to fit him into a completely consistent scheme of analysis.

The soul and the body are one. This fact is more perfectly expressed in the more primitive psychology of the Hebrews than in the more advanced philosophy of the Greeks. The Hebrews conceived the soul, significantly, as residing in the blood. They did not even distinguish sharply between "soul" and "life" and expressed both connotations in several words, all of which had an original connotation of "breath." This unity of soul and body does not deny the human capacity for freedom. It does not reduce man to the processes of nature in which he stands, though yet he stands above them. It merely insists on the organic unity between the two. The mind of man never functions as if it were discarnate. That is, it is not only

293

subject to the limitations of a finite perspective but also to the necessities of physical existence.

This very dependence of the soul upon the body might suggest that the finiteness of the body is the chief source of the corruption of the soul. It is because the mind looks out upon the world from two eyes, limited in their range, that it cannot see as far as it would like. And it is because rational processes are related to natural necessities that the mind is tempted to exchange its ideal of a disinterested contemplation of existence for the task of special pleading in the interests of the body in which it is incarnate. But to explain human evil in these terms is to forget that there is no sin in nature. Animals live in the harmony assigned to them by nature. If this harmony is not perfect and sets species against species in the law of the jungle, no animal ever aggravates, by his own decision, the disharmonies which are, with restricted harmonies, the condition of its life.

The root of sin is in spirit and not in nature. The assertion of that fact distinguishes Christianity both from naturalism, which denies the reality of sin, and from various types of mysticism and dualism, which think that finiteness as such, or in other words the body, is the basis of evil. Even when sin is not selfishness but sensuality, man's devotion to his physical life and to sense enjoyments differs completely from animal normality. It is precisely because he is free to centre his life in certain physical processes and to lift them out of the harmonious relationships in which nature has them, that man falls into sin. In the first chapter of Paul's Epistle to the Romans he accurately defines sin, first, as the egotism by which man changes "the glory of the uncorruptible God into an image made like to corruptible man." But he continues by suggesting that sensuality is a further development in the nature of sin, "Wherefore God also gave them up to uncleanness through the lusts of their own hearts, to dishonour their own bodies between themselves." Whatever the relation of sensuality and selfishness in the realm of human evil, whether they are two types of sin or whether one is derived from the other, it is obvious that both are the fruits of the spirit and not of the flesh.

It is, of course, true that the peculiar situation in which man stands, of being a finite and physical creature and yet gifted to survey eternity, is a temptation to sin. The persistency of sin is probably derived from the perennial force of this temptation. When man looks at himself and makes himself an object of his own thought he finds himself to be merely one of many creatures in creation. But when he looks at the world he finds his own mind the focusing center of the whole. When man acts he confuses these two visions of himself. He knows that he ought to act so as to assume only his rightful place in the harmony of

295

the whole. But his actual action is always informed by the ambition to make himself the centre of the whole. Thus he is betrayed into egotism. Quite rightly St. Paul suggests that, once he has destroyed his relation to the divine centre and source of life, man may go further and centre his life in some particular process of his own life rather than his own life in its totality. In fact, the second step is inevitable. Since the real self is related organically to the whole of life, it is disturbed in its own unity when it seeks to make itself the centre and disturbs the unity of life. Thus sin lies at the juncture of nature and spirit.

If it is untrue that the body is of itself evil while the soul or the spirit is good, it follows that the highest moral ideal is not one of ascetic flagellation of the flesh but of a physical and spiritual existence in which mind and body serve each other. Browning was right in the anti-asceticism expressed in *Rabbi Ben Ezra:*

"To man, propose this test—
The body at its best,
How far can that project thy soul on its lone way?

.   .   .   .

Let us not always say
'Spite of this flesh to-day
I strove, made head, gained ground upon the whole!'
As the bird wings and sings,
Let us cry 'All good things
Are ours, nor soul helps flesh more, now, than flesh
    helps soul!' "

296

The possibilities of the fulfilment of this life transcend our experience not because the soul is immortal
and the body is mortal but because this human life,
soul and body, is both immersed in flux and above it,
and because it involves itself in sin in this unique position from which there is no escape by its own powers.
The fulfilment of life beyond the possibilities of this
existence is a justified hope, because of our human
situation, that is, because a life which knows the flux
in which it stands cannot be completely a part of that
flux. On the other hand this hope is not one which fulfils itself by man's own powers. God must complete
what remains incomplete in human existence. This is
true both because there is no simple division in human
life between what is mortal and what is immortal so
that the latter could slough off the former; and because the incompleteness of human life is not only
finiteness but sin.

II

The hope of resurrection of the body is preferable
to the idea of the immortality of the soul because it
expresses at once a more individual and a more social
idea of human existence. Human life has a paradoxical relation not only to nature but to human history.
Each individual is a product of the social forces of
human history and achieves his significance in relating

297

himself to them. Most ideals of personal immortality are highly individualistic. They interpret the meaning of life in such a way that the individual is able to think of ultimate fulfilment without any reference to the social process of which he is a part. This process is interpreted in purely negative terms. It is merely a part of the whole world of mortality which the immortal soul sloughs off. In contrast to such an interpretation, it is significant that the biblical idea of the resurrection grew out of a social hope. The Messianic kingdom was conceived of as the fulfilment of a social process, first of all, of course, as the fulfilment of the life of Israel. The idea of individual resurrection arose first in relation to this hope. The righteous would be resurrected to participate in this ultimate triumph. The idea of a social fulfilment was consequently basic. Not only individual life, but the whole development of the human race was understood as standing under the curious paradox of pointing to goals which transcended the possibilities of finite existence. Social history, in other words, was a meaningful process to the prophets of Israel. Protestant Christianity has usually been too individualistic to understand this religious appreciation of the meaning of social processes. In consequence, the liberal idea of progress as the meaning of history and the Marxian idea of a revolution which will usher in a fulfilled history are justified protests against Protestant Christian individualism. They are both mistaken in not taking the idea of resurrection seriously enough. They think it is possible for a history, involved in the conditions and contingencies of nature, to overcome these by some final act of mind or will and establish a conditionless goodness in human history. Their Utopia is, in other words, the Kingdom of God minus the resurrection, that is minus the divine transformation of human existence. But whatever the defects in these social conceptions, they restore an important element to prophetic religion. Any religion which thinks only in terms of individual fulfilment also thinks purely in terms of the meaning of individual life. But man's body is the symbol of his organic relationship to the processes of history. Each life may have a significance which transcends the social process but not one which can be developed without reference to that process.

In the Cromwellian Revolution a great many sects sprang up, Levellers, Diggers and Anabaptists, who insisted on this old prophetic hope of the Kingdom of God in contrast to the individualism of the churches in which there was no appreciation of the meaning of history. These sectaries felt that the revolution in which they were involved had a religious significance and pointed toward a society in which the hopes of brotherhood and justice would be fulfilled. Significantly one of the best thinkers of this sectarian movement, a man named Overton, spent time and effort to refute the idea of immortality and establish the conception of the resurrection. It is not apparent from his writings that he consciously connected the idea of resurrection with his social hopes. But it is significant that he had this interest. The idea of resurrection is a rebuke and a correction of all too individualistic conceptions of religion. This individualism is always a luxury of the more privileged and comfortable classes who do not feel the frustrations of society sufficiently to be prompted to a social hope and who are not in such organic relation to their fellows as to understand the meaning of life in social terms

It is true of course that modern men express their social hope in terms other than that of the idea of the resurrection. They are either liberals who believe in progress, or radicals who believe in a classless society on the other side of a revolution. But this secularisation is no advance. It is not, as assumed, a substitution of superior scientific ideas for outmoded religious myths. It is rather the proof of modern man's blindness to the paradoxes of human existence. He does not understand the hopes of an unconditioned perfection, both social and individual, which beckon the human conscience and which are involved in every concept of the relative and the historical good. He sees them in history but does not see that they point beyond history.

III

Strangely enough, and yet not strange to those who think profoundly upon the question, the body is the mark of individuality as well as of sociality. Pure nature does not, of course, produce individuals. It produces types, species and genera. The individuality of human life is the product of freedom; and freedom is the fruit of the spirit. Yet pure spirit is pure mind and pure mind is universal. Pure mind expresses itself in the universally valid concepts of mathematics and logic. These concepts are universal because they are forms without content. That is why "spiritual" religions, which may begin with a great degree of individualism than more earthy and social religions, end by losing the soul in some eternal and divine unity. All consistent mysticism (which does not include most Christian mysticism which is not consistent) regards individuality, egohood, as of itself evil. If Christian mysticism is not consistent upon this point that is due to the fact that Christianity, no matter how greatly influenced by more dualistic thought, never completely escapes the biblical ideas of the goodness of creation and the resurrection of the body.

The fact is that individuality and individualisation are the product of human history; and human history is a pattern which is woven upon a loom in which the necessities of nature and the freedom of the spirit are both required. Perhaps it would be more exact to describe one as the loom and the other as the shuttle. Whenever the significance of history is depreciated the ultimate consequence is also a depreciation of individuality.

To believe that the *body* is resurrected is to say, therefore, that eternity is not a cancellation of time and history but that history is fulfilled in eternity. But to insist that the body must be *resurrected* is to understand that time and history have meaning only as they are borne by an eternity which transcends them. They could in fact not be at all without that eternity. For history would be meaningless succession without the eternal purpose which bears it.

The idea of the fulfilment of life is very difficult, partly because of the dialectical relation of time and eternity and partly because of the dialectical relation of the individual to society. The old classical idealism resolved the difficulties by denying the significance of time and history; and modern naturalism seeks to resolve it by seeking to make time and history self-sufficing. The naturalists divide themselves into individualists and communists. The former destroy the dialectical and organic relation of the individual to his society and produce discrete individuals who have no interest in society or history. The communists on the other hand think it possible to offer the individual a satisfactory hope of fulfilment in terms of an ideal society. They do not understand that individual life always transcends the social process as well as being fulfilled in it. This will be true in the most ideal society. There are aspects of meaning in individual life which will escape the appreciation of even the most just society; and there are hopes of fulfilment which transcend the power of any society to realise.

The very genesis of the idea of resurrection lay in this dilemma. The great prophetic movement in Israel promised the fulfilment of Israel's hopes. But what would become of the individuals who perished before those hopes were realised? The question is put searchingly in one of the great apocalyptic books, Fourth Ezra: "Lo, Lord thou art ready to meet with thy blessing those that survive to the end; but what shall our predecessors do, or we ourselves or our posterity? Couldst thou not have created them all at once, those that are, and those that shall be?" Or again in the same book: "What does it profit us that there is promised us an imperishable hope whereas we are so miserably brought to futility?"

Here is a very legitimate individualism. Social and political religions which do not understand it, stand on the level of Hebraic prophecy before the idea of the resurrection of the body answered those questions. It is an individualism which must emerge whenever human culture is profound enough to measure the full depth of human freedom. At such a time it becomes apparent that each individual transcends society too much to be able to regard it either as his judge or as his redeemer. He faces God rather than society and he may have to defy society in the name of God.

If an adequate prophetic religion expresses the real relation of the individual and society in terms of a hope of fulfilment in which the individual is resurrected to participate in the fulfilment of society, such a conception is rationally just as difficult as the idea of resurrection itself. The former seems to take no account of a society continually involved in flux just as the latter seems to defy the inevitability of mortality in nature. But that merely means that such a religion is expressing the idea that history is more than flux and that nature is not just mortality. Here, once more, religion is involved in myth as a necessary symbol of its faith.

It is important not to press the myth of the resurrection to yield us too detailed knowledge of the future. "It doth not yet appear what we shall be." Every effort to describe the details of fulfilment and to give plans and specifications of the heavenly city leads to absurdity. Such efforts have in fact encouraged the modern man to reject all conceptions either of individual fulfilment or of a Kingdom of God which fulfils the whole human enterprise. But it is instructive that these disavowals of mythical absurdities have tempted modern men to curious rational absurdities. Among the greatest of these is to revel in the relativities of historical flux and yet nourish a covert hope that history, as it is, will finally culminate by its own processes into something which is not history but a realm of unconditioned goodness. Every one who rejects the basic conceptions, implicit in the idea of the resurrection, is either a moral nihilist or an utopian, covert or overt. Since there are few moral nihilists, it follows that most moderns are utopians. Imagining themselves highly sophisticated in their emancipation from religion, they give themselves to the most absurd hopes about the possibilities of man's natural history.

It is significant that there is no religion, or for that matter no philosophy of life, whether explicit or implicit, which does not hold out the hope of the fulfilment of life in some form or other. Since it is man's nature to be emancipated of the tyranny of the immediate present and to transcend the processes of nature in which he is involved, he cannot exist without having his eyes upon the future. The future is the symbol of his freedom.

The Christian view of the future is complicated by the realization of the fact that the very freedom which brings the future into view has been the occasion for the corruption of the present in the heart of man. Mere development of what he now is cannot save man, for development will heighten all the contradictions in which he stands. Nor will emancipation from the law of development and the march of time through entrance into a timeless and motionless eternity save him. That could only annihilate him. His hope consequently lies in a forgiveness which will overcome not his finiteness but his sin, and a divine omnipotence which will complete his life without destroying its essential nature. Hence the final expression of hope in the Apostolic Creed: "I believe in the forgiveness of sins, the resurrection of the body and life everlasting" is a much more sophisticated expression of hope in ultimate fulfilment than all of its modern substitutes. It grows out of a realization of the total human situation which the modern mind has not fathomed. The symbols by which this hope is expressed are, to be sure, difficult. The modern mind imagines that it has rejected the hope because of this difficulty. But the real cause of the rejection lies in its failure to understand the problem of human existence in all its complexity.